Mathias Jansson

Everything I Shoot Is Art

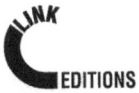

LINK EDITIONS

LINK Editions

Domenico Quaranta, *In Your Computer*, 2011
Valentina Tanni, *Random*, 2011
Miltos Manetas, *In My Computer – Miltos Manetas*, 2011
Gene McHugh, *Post Internet*, 2011
Domenico Quaranta (ed.), *Collect the WWWorld. The Artist as Archivist in the Internet Age*, 2011. Exhibition Catalogue. Texts by Josephine Bosma, Gene McHugh, Joanne McNeil, Domenico Quaranta
Brad Troemel, *Peer Pressure*, 2011
Domenico Quaranta (ed.), *Gazira Babeli,* 2011
Yves Bernard, Domenico Quaranta (eds.), *Holy Fire. Art of the Digital Age*, 2011
Kevin Bewersdorf, *Spirit Surfing*, 2012

Mathias Jansson
Everything I Shoot Is Art

Publisher: LINK Editions, Brescia 2012
www.linkartcenter.eu

Printed and distributed by: Lulu.com
www.lulu.com

ISBN 978-1-291-02050-2

«*I see freedom in the chaos of the unestablished.*»

_ Sachiko Hayashi, 2012

Mathias Jansson is a Swedish art critic and researcher. He writes about New Media Art and Game Art for blogs and magazines such as Gamescenes, Digimag and Next Level. His main body of work consists of a huge corpus of interviews with the pioneers of Game Art, as well as critics, curators and gallery owners operating in the field of Game Art. www.janssonswebb.se

Contents

Preface

There is a preconception about artists and new technologies. People usually believe that artists are introvert and not so much concerned with what happens around them in the world. And when it comes to innovations and new technologies, well, let's say that artists are not really up to date. I mean – do they really know what an iPhone is?

This is – of course – an old Romantic idea, that has nothing to do with the modern and contemporary artist. On the contrary, if you look back to history, you will find that artists have always been the first adopters of new technologies, and they have always been able to use them in innovative, unconventional ways.

When, at the beginning of the XIX century, photography was invented, it didn't take long before artist started to experiment with this new medium. The same happened with cinema at the end of the XIX century, and with television and video in the sixties. Today, people from the movie industries and advertising companies are often imitating and getting inspirations from artists, as the more updated and innovative users of their media.

A similar scenario can be found when it comes to new technologies like computers, mobile phones and the internet. There is this 1986 video featuring Andy Warhol "painting" Debbie Harry with an Amiga computer. Of course, the Amiga people were well aware that artists like Andy Warhol were very interested in using new technologies to make art, but they were also aware of the common preconception about artists and new technologies. So, the promotional message of this video was: if an artist like Andy Warhol can use it, well, it should be really easy to use.

But this is – of course – another false assumption. Along the last years, I have seen artists doing things with computers and video games that show an high level of ability and skills, uncommon between the average users.

In the late sixties a new medium was born which would change the whole entertainment industry. It all started with two white rectangles and a white square, that should be interpreted as symbols for two rackets and a ball. It was the fist video game, and it was called "Tennis for Two", but it became famous under the commercial name "Pong". Since the sixties, the video game industry has exploded, and it has affected our culture in many ways. There we can find a new generation of artists experimenting and using video games in innovative ways to make art.

One point with this book is to show that artists are often the most updated and innovative when it comes to explore and use new media as video games, computers and the internet. In this volume I collected essays and interviews with artists and game designers that are using video games in ways that we could describe as art. Because video games have the potential, like film and literature, to be much more than just fun and entertainment: they can be art.

Mathias Jansson, August 2012

ESSAYS

Confessions of a Game Art Addict

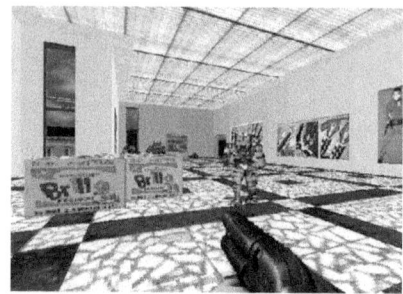

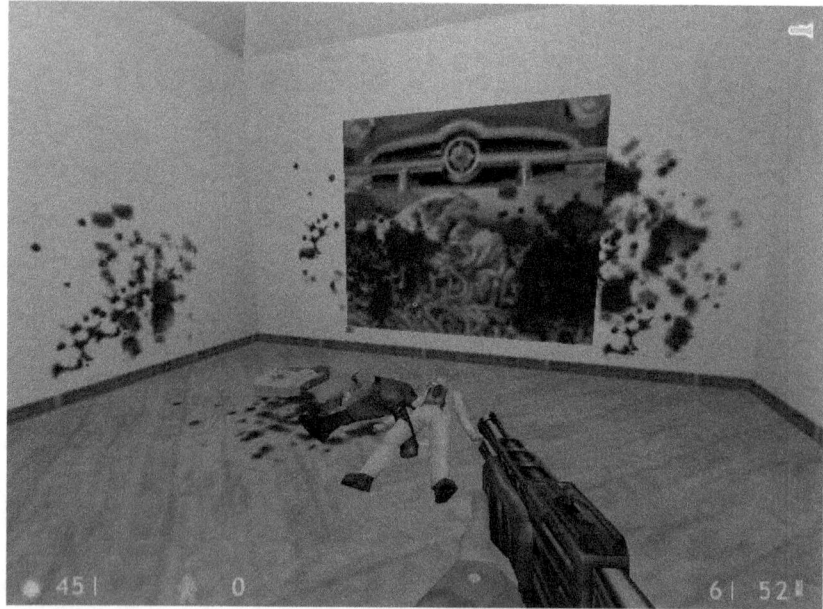

Tobias Bernstrup, Palle Torsson, *Museum Meltdown*, 1996 – 1999. Above: screen shot from The Contemporary Art Centre of Vilnius, 1997; below: screen shot from The Modern Museum, Stockholm 1999. Images courtesy the artists

Like a punch in the solar plexus of fine art: that's what it felt like six years ago, when I stumbled upon the piece *Museum Meltdown* by the Swedish artists Palle Torsson and Tobias Bernstrup. *Museum Meltdown* is a series of three artistically modified video games based on reconstructions of famous art museums. The first piece was created in 1996, when both artists were still studying at the art school. *Museum Meltdown #1* is a reconstruction of the Arken Museum of Modern Art outside Copenhagen – built with the help of the classic video game Duke Nukem. In a new level added to the game, you can run around the museum, shoot monsters, and destroy art. I found the combination of video games and art, popular culture and fine art, violence and destruction in contrast to the typical silence of the exhibition hall fascinating. The fact that there has been relatively little written about video games and art is the main reason that I have followed this path for the last six years.

But I must confess that I myself am not a gamer. I played video games when I was young, as many in my generation did, but as an adult I don't really have time and I find most of the games boring. The concepts haven't changed since I was young: shoot, kill, hit, jump, run, collect and solve puzzles. The graphics and sound qualities are now better of course, but the games themselves usually aren't. Instead, I prefer to investigate and write about how artists are using video games to create art.

When I grew up in the 1980s, video games and heavy metal music were considered by adults and established society to be low and "dangerous" forms of popular culture. For me, artworks like *Museum Meltdown* were a revelation: this new creative and artistic medium that had for so long been looked down upon, even despised by the art world, was now being exhibited in established art museums. Video games were finally being taken seriously, and they were kicking the art world's ass. You could now enter an art museum with a gun and blow art history to pieces – virtually, anyway. In some sense, works like *Museum Meltdown* remind me of the 1909 "Futurist Manifesto" which declared: "We want to demolish museums and libraries." With this video game, you could do so, at least with a virtual copy of the art museum.

So: when did artists start to use video games to make art? You can find the prehistory of Game Art in the demoscene, which was developed during the eighties when different hacker and cracker groups made "intros" to video games after "cracking" their copyright protection. To show the world who was the cracker and what an excellent programmer she was, they created audio-visual intros which tried to squeeze the most advanced effects out of their processors. These creative and artistic short demos were the first attempt to combine video games with artistic expression.

Two pioneers in the field that must also be mentioned are both women, working within a genre that in the beginning was largely dominated by men. In Jane Veeder's *VIZGAME* (1985), the player can create his or her own real-time animation. The program was created by Jane Veeder in 1985 and runs on a Datamax UV-1 Graphics System. Also, Suzanne Treister in the late eighties painted game-inspired paintings, and in the nineties created a series of fictional video game stills using Amiga's Deluxe Paint II.

The first traces of Game Art on the international art scene can be found in 1993, at the 45th Venice Biennale. There, the Chinese artist Feng Mengbo exhibited art from his *The Video Endgame Series*: a series of acrylic-on-canvas paintings in which he mixed images from the Culture Revolution (1966-1976) with his childhoods memories of playing 8-bit video games. Another early Game Art project by Mengbo was *Game Over: Long March* (1994), a set of 42 acrylic-on-canvas paintings. Around 2000 Mengbo started to work with modification of video games and created his own interactive video-game installation. *Long March: Restart* (2008) is probably the best known: a large-scale interactive video-game installation which was acquired by the New York MoMA in 2010 for its collection.

Another international breakthrough for Game Art as a new art form was established in 1995 when the Austrian artist Orhan Kipcak exhibited *ArsDoom* at Ars Electronica in Linz, Austria. The artwork was a modified copy of the game Doom II with a reconstruction of the Brucknerhaus' exhibition hall. During the first years of Game Art most works set out to modify famous commercial First Person Shooter (FPS) games like Doom, Unreal, and Quake, which had tools that made it easy for users to design new levels and thus modify the games. I've identified a particular genre of Game Art that I call First Museum Shooters. As in the examples of *ArsDoom* and *Museum Meltdown*, First Museum Shooters are reconstructions of famous exhibition spaces were the player can run around and shoot monsters and, in the process, destroy the exhibited art.

This early artistic experiments with video games were at the time not so different from hacks and mods made by gamers around the world. The genre "First Person Shooter" had literally exploded with Doom and, as with Doom, these new games were often shipped with simple tools to create new levels, characters and settings for the games. When Anne-Marie Schleiner curated the exhibition "Cracking the Maze: Game Plug-ins and Patches as Hacker Art" in 1999, it included not only artists but also regular players who had hacked and modified video games. One year earlier, Konrad Becker had launched the exhibition "Synreal: The Unreal Modification" at Institut für Neue Kulturtechnologien in Wien.

"Synreal" was an exhibition based on modifications of the popular Unreal games. Unreal became a very popular video game for artists due to its graphic engine that was very easy to modify with the help of several tools. The close connection between artistic modifications and regular player's modification is probably one explanation for why this new art form didn't make it on the international art scene in the beginning. At the time there was still big skepticism towards video game culture. In media, video games were usually described as new mass entertainment filled with violence, gore and blood, unhealthy and dangerous for youths. The idea that it could be used to create art was still far away.

In 2002, Game Art enters Documenta for the first time. It was again Feng Mengbo who broke down the institutional wall presenting at Documenta 11 his work *Q4U*, a modification of the game Quake. Next step in this slow process of recognition in the art world was the Whitney Biennal 2004, were two works of Game Art were put on show. The first was *Velvet Strike*, by Anne-Marie Schleiner, Joan Leandre and Brody Condon: a graffiti add-on to Counterstrike, which made it possible to spray anti-war messages in war game. The other was *Super Mario Clouds* by Cory Arcangel, a hacked NES cartridge where the artist removed every graphic object except the scrolling white clouds. Now a classic, the work has been later included in the Whitney museum collection.

After 2005 the number of exhibitions including Game Art increases and the interest for video games and art is shown by a number of books, articles and seminars. At the time the artists mostly abandoned game modification and started to explore and mix video games with other art forms like performance, installation, video and machinima, paintings, sculpture and so on.

Between 2007 and 2008, the LABoral Art and Industrial Creation Centre in Gijon, Spain, presented an ambitious project: a trilogy of exhibitions called "GameWorld", "Playware" and "Homo Ludens Ludens" that focused on expressions of play in contemporary culture, including video games and art. All together, these exhibitions made an important summary of the developments of Game Art until 2008 and showed that video games were now taken seriously in the art world.

Over the last years we have seen a growing interest from institutions and museums for video games as art. In March 2013 The Smithsonian Art Museum in Washington D.C will open an exhibition called "The Art of Videogame", which is described as "the first exhibition to explore the forty-year evolution of video games as an artistic medium, with a focus on striking visual effects and the creative use of new technologies."

19 years after Feng Mengbo participation in the Venice Biennal, video games returned to the 54th Venice Biennale with the exhibition "Neoludica: Art is a game 2011-1966", with Deborah Ferrari as chief curator. "Neoludica" included six different exhibitions with 34 artists, some well known in the new media art scene like Tale of Tales, Miltos Manetas, Eva & Franco Mattes and Molleindustria.

Today, Game Art has become a broad category that includes Art Games, installations, machinima, paintings and sculpture. If I were to try and define Game Art, I would say that the definition you can find in the book *GameScenes: Art in the Age of video games* (Johan & Levi, Milan 2006), edited by Matteo Bittanti and Domenico Quaranta, is still the best:

> Game Art is any art in which digital games played a significant role in the creation, production, and/or display of the artwork. The resulting artwork can exist as a game, painting, photography, sound, animation, video, performance or gallery installation.

A shorter version of this text has been formerly published in *Art 21* in January 2012.

Insert Art to Play

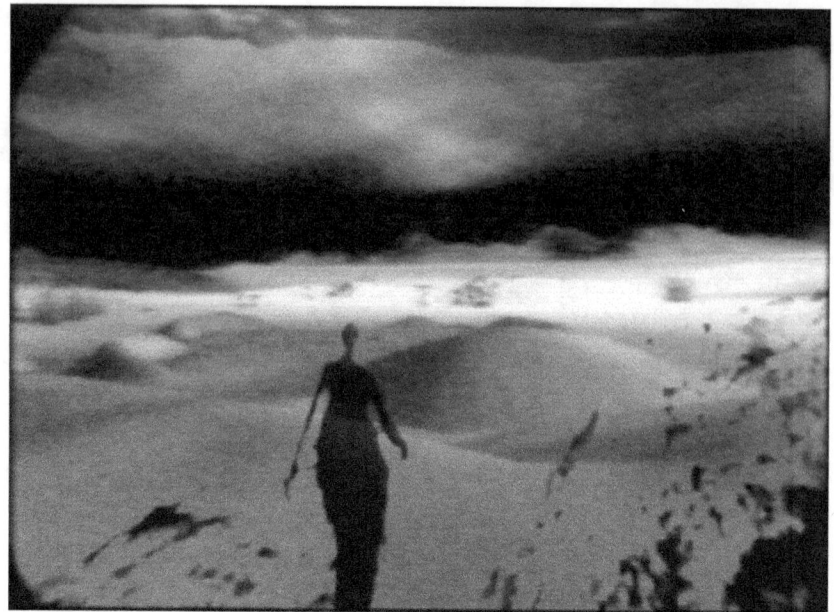

Bill Viola, *The Night Journey,* 2005 – 2008. Screenshot, © 2005-2008 University of Southern California

The Artist Is Present is a performance by Marina Abramović, performed at the Museum of Modern Art in New York in 2010. People queued for hours in front of the museum to sit a couple of minutes in front of the artist. The god-like "presence" of the artist in the exhibition was the performance. It gave the visitor a chance to cross eyes with the Artist, but it was a silent performance where you couldn't ask anything to Abramović.

In 2011, game designer Pippin Barr did a game with the same name of Abramović's performance. The German newspaper *Die Spiegel* reviewed it as the most boring game in the world. Why? Because nothing happens in the game? Because it's a game about waiting, like Samuel Beckett's drama *Waiting for Godot*?

If you see *The Artist Is Present* only as a video game, then I agree with you – it's definitely boring. But if you, on the other hand, look at it as a piece of art, well – then it's brilliant. Pippin Barr explains in the interview featured in this book:

Waiting is such a no-no in games (Narthex is a notable exception and there are others, like Desert Bus), it's regarded as so abusive, and yet it's a major part of life. To the extent we want games to (sometimes) be "about life", waiting is fair game.

But Pippin Barr is not an artist; I would rather say he is an indie game designer making small games in 8-bit retro graphics. The games are very easy to play, but often impossible to win, if you can even win. In the game *Ancient Greek Punishment* you can play as Sisyphus, Tantalus, Prometheus or some other characters from the Greek mythology that, for their crimes against the gods, were punished to eternally repeat the same gesture. Since the punishment is eternal you cannot win – you are predestined to fail. But even when you know that you cannot win, you will play it again and again. In some way we humans always believe that we can defeat the system by intelligence, endurance or by cheating. When you remove the possibility to win or even making progress in the game, is it still a game, or is it art?

There are now lots of video games that are not for entertainment in the first place. They are often collected under the category serious games, i.e. games with an agenda, games that will affect you and tell you something. They can be commercial games, documentary, propaganda, or educational games. But there is also a category which we use to call "art games". So what is the definition of an art game? Well, as all good art, an art game questions, explores and stretches the boundaries of you experience. Art games can look like a game, but they are often unplayable, and more generally work in the opposite way of what you expect from a game. An art game is more than some hours of mind-blowing hilarious fun. Like all good art, it should affect you and makes you reflect and think in new and different ways. An art game tells you something about being a human. It can refer to existential, religious or psychological issues.

When we talk about art games, we often mean games that are created by artists or exhibited in an art context, but with that definition in mind, a lot of interesting, truly "artistic" games fall outside the art game genre. Take Pippin Barr, for example. Barr is not an artist, but since the game is about a famous art performance it was soon recognized by the art scene and also exhibited in a museum context. But still, there are lots of other game designers that have been never discovered by the art scene, though their works are very close to what we mean for art.

It's time to start looking at the medium as a means for artistic expression, instead of looking at where its creator locates herself in the creative arena, or where the artefact has been exhibited. Along the last years, there have been an intensive debate concerning whether video games should be considered art or not. For me, the answer is pretty easy. I use to compare video games with movies. At the beginning of the century, cinema wasn't considered an art form. It was a new dangerous medium that ruined the youth with sex and violence and should be banned. The same argument has been used against video games. But along the century, cinema developed and won recognition as a high art form. Today there are lot of directors (think about Ingmar Bergman, Federico Fellini, Peter Greenaway, just to name a few) that are considered great artists in their field. We also looked back to the pioneers of the moving images as Georges Méliès, D. W. Griffith and Sergei Eisenstein and celebrate them as groundbreaking artists. Maybe we'll do the same with the pioneers of video games in the future? But of course, not all films are art, as well as not all music is art, not all drama is art, not all novels are art. Many video games, films, books etc. are just made to entertain you, but this doesn't prevent some of them to be really good art. As always with art, you can't extend the art label to every use of the medium, but you have to look at the context and the contents.

Earlier in this text, I mentioned Samuel Beckett's play *Waiting for Godot* (1953). It can be hard to believe that a absurd drama about waiting for a person that never arrives could be translated into a video game. Yet, Swedish artist Olle Essvik did it, adapting and updating Samuel Beckett's plays *Waiting for Godot* and *Endgame* (1957) for the digital age. In his words [1], his game *Waiting For* (2011) is:

> A theatrical play with a number of set instructions constantly repeated, but each time in a different order. The piece consists of a programmed and interactive animation sequence shown online and resembling a computer game, but where the concept has been expanded and the actual game element have been left out.

To translate a book or a play into an art game is not uncommon, as in Tracy Fullerton's game *Walden* after Henry David Thoreau's book written in 1855. The game follows the plot in the book as the player plays the role of Thoreau. He has to build a cabin, collect food, fuel, shelter and clothing to survive. The development team of the game also did a database with all the plants and animals Thoreau mentions in the book, that you can explore and use. *Walden* looks like a clone of The Sims, or of The Settlers series, where you have to build up a living from scratch based on your skills and on what you can find in nature. Thoreau's two years stay in the forest of Walden was an experiment: he wanted to show the world that live in harmony with nature was still possible, and sustainable. I suppose we would call it a retreat today – when you escape the stress of the world and find yourself in a spiritual way in the nature. In the game, you are rewarded when you enjoy solitude, listening to the sounds of nature or reading. In some ways, the Walden experience is an inner journey, back to what really counts in life.

Another game that's also about a journey is Bill Viola's *The Night Journey* (2005 - 2008), a project in which Tracy Fullerton was also involved. Just like *Walden, The Night Journey* is a game that rewards you to take it slow and to be introspective. In the words of Bill Viola:

> You're alone and you're not even told why you're there. You just fall out of the sky into the middle of this amazing landscape with mountains, sea, desert, and forest, and go wherever you want. [2]

As *The Artist is Present* and *Walden, The Night Journey* is an anti-game. If in ordinary games you are rewarded when you rush through the game as fast as possible to collect coins or shoot people, here you are rewarded when you take it easy and slow. All these games are about an inner journey, in some sense to find yourself, to be aware of the small things around you.

A slow year (2010), by Ian Bogost, is also about inner reflection and slowness. It consists of four games, one for each season. "These games are neither action nor strategy: each of them requires a different kind of sedate observation and methodical input" [3]. According to the author, they are "game poems" about the shifting season. There's no story and no goal in the games. It's more about experiencing a feeling, a mood. They could also bee seen as a metaphor for the cycle of life with birth, growth, fading and death.

Life and death are also core issues of Tales of Tales' art game *The Graveyard* (2008). The plot is pretty simple: you play an old woman with a stick walking up the gravel path on a churchyard. Your goal is a bench at the end of the path where you can sit down and listen to a song and remember you life. In most games you should avoid death but in *The Graveyard* it's the opposite – the goal of the game is to die in peace. *The Graveyard* is a memento mori in the form of a game. Another interesting thing in the work is that the main character is not a young athletic muscular hero with superpowers, but an old harmless lady.

The meaning of life is a theme that you can find in many art games, as in Molleindustria's *Every day the same dream* (2009). We are all familiar with the grey every day, when the alarm bell rings very early in the morning, you have to get up, get dress, eat, and go to work. In Molleindustria's game you play the grey everyday, with the alternative option to rebel and suicide when you get bored of it. *Every day the same dream* is a short game about repetitions. It's just one day in an average human's life, but it captures the essential of life. In the movie *Groundhog Day* (1993), actor Bill Murray plays the misanthropic TV weatherman Phil Connors assigned to cover the annual Groundhog festivities in the small Hick town of Punxsutawney. Suddenly a snow blizzard makes it impossible to leave the town and the team has to stay overnight. When Phil wakes is the morning, it is the same day as before. *Groundhog Day* is very similar to a video game. Phil has to live / play the same day / level over and over again, trying to learn how he will handle it to become a better human so he can go on to the next day, or level if you prefer. *Every day the same dream* is based on the same concept. By repetition of one single day we can learn to handle and change our life into something better.

Jason Rohrer also made a short game about life called *Passage* (2007). In the game you metaphorically walk through life moving from left to right. In the beginning you can choose if you should fall in love or not. *Passage* is simple and made with 8-bit retro graphic, but again it captures the essence of life. We are born, meet someone we love or not, and in a very short time we make our passage through life.

You can choose to read a book by Franz Kafka, look at a painting by Francis Bacon, see a play by Arthur Miller, listen to a concert by Stravinsky, see a film by Ingmar Bergman or play a video game to experience what it's like to be a human. But don't let the medium confuse you or restrict your experience. The medium is not the message, as Marshall McLuhan phrased. The message is always what counts in art, regardless what medium you are using. And the medium can well be a video game.

[1] Artist's statement, online at http://jimpalt.org/waitingfor/.
[2] Hilarie M. Sheets, "Click Here For Enlightenment", in *Art News*, April 2010.
[3] Artist's statement, online at
www.bogost.com/games/game_poems.shtml.

From Plaintext Players to Avatar Actors: A Short Survey of Online Gaming Performance

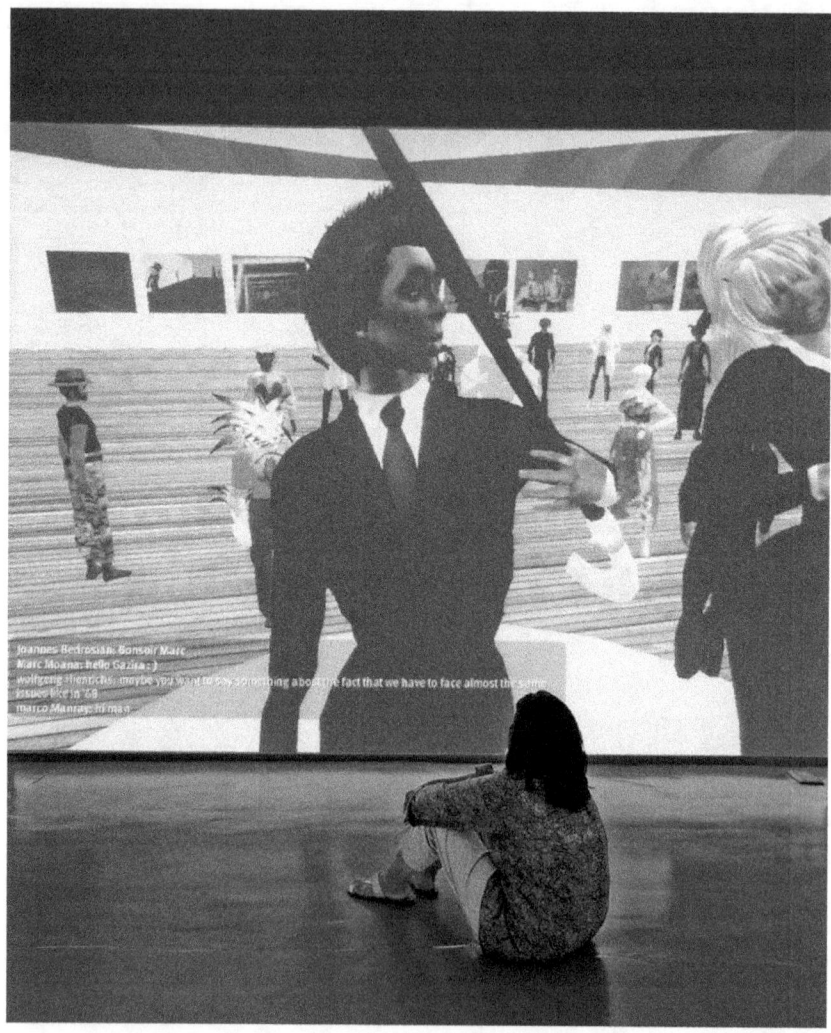

Eva and Franco Mattes aka 0100101110101101.org, *Reenactment of Gilbert&George's The Singing Sculpture*, 2007-10. Online performance. Exhibition view, Galerie Mirchandani+Steinruecke Gallery, Mumbai. Image courtesy the artists.

Performance art emerged in the mid sixties into the seventies and was a way to push the boundaries between art and everyday life. Many artists saw performance as an opportunity to bring art directly to the audience without having to detour through the galleries, curators or agents. Performance therefore often occurs outside the institutions on streets, squares or other public places. It was defined as an antithesis to theatre and the ideal was to "create an ephemeral and authentic experience for performer and audience in an event that could not be repeated, captured or purchased." [1] Famous performance artists of this time are Yoko Ono, Joseph Beuys, Vito Acconci, Chris Burden and Marina Abramović.

With that background, it's not surprising that performance artists today explore computer games and online worlds. These new digital worlds give the artists an opportunity to meet a new audience and bring their art into people's living rooms. With the help of the internet they can also reach a new and broader art public all around the world.

Online performance started in the early text based systems known as MOO, MUD and in chat rooms, and followed the technology development into 3D online worlds. One thing that surprised me when I started doing this survey was that so many artists have chosen to re-enact famous performances from the history of art in different video games and on-line worlds. To be witty you could say that many of these old performances have got a second life in Second Life.

Antoinette LaFarge

One of the first attempts to explore performance on-line was made by Antoinette LaFarge, an American artist and professor of Digital Media at the University of California Irvine. In 1994 she founded the Plaintext Players, an online performance group inspired by MOO. MOO (a cousin to MUD – Multi-User Dungeon) was a system used to create online text-based adventure games in the beginning of the nineties. In an interview I did with Antoinette LaFarge for *Gamescenes* in October 2011 she told me how she got involved in MOO performances in the beginning:

> I got involved with MOOs in early 1994 while I was in graduate school. I was initially entranced by the immersive quality of these spaces and the way they straddled a line between performing and being, and between writing and doing. From the outset I had a strong impulse to play in MOO, to make up stuff, to not take part under my own name and history. Some

of my fellow students had a similar impulse, and at first we would just meet up online and improvise very loosely. For instance, we might change our avatar names (@rename) 4 or 5 times an hour just to prod each other to change how we were interacting. We were the puppetmasters and the puppets. [2]

The first performance by Plaintext Players was called *Christmas* and was a series that took place online on PMC MOO between the first of March and the 18th December 1994. The series was based on a scenario by Robert Allen featuring the archetypal character trio: Big Man, Little Man, and Bloody Zelda. During the year when the series run, the ill-assorted trio found themselves in court, in hell, and lost in the desert as they played out their struggles.

Joseph DeLappe

During the nineties the online game world was rapidly changing from text based adventure games into action games with 3D graphic worlds. The game Doom (1993) started the new popular genre of First Person Shooters, and the multi-player mode was a precursor to many on-line games in the genre. In the middle of the nineties, with the expansion of Internet, on-line gaming became a more and more popular occupation for gamers. These new scenarios opened up new opportunities for artists. One of the pioneers in this context is the American artist Joseph DeLappe, who started with online gaming performance in 2001:

It was in the spring of 2001 that I engaged in my first online gaming performance – *Howl: Elite Force Voyager Online*. I entered the game as Allen Ginsberg and proceeded to perform the entirety of his seminal beat poem *Howl*, word for word. [3]

Many of DeLappe's works have an anti-war theme. In the war game Medal of Honor: Allied Assault he mixed an antiwar message with poetry. He logged into the game and started to read poetry by the war poet Siegfried Sassoon by typing the poems in the games chat field. Sassoon was a British poet who wrote satirical anti-war poetry during World War One.

DeLappe's most notable work is otherwise a performance that began in March 2006 on the third anniversary of the Iraq war. *Dead-in-iraq* is the title of the work but also DeLappe's alias when he logs in to the game America's Army. America's Army is an online game that functions as a recruitment platform for the U.S. military. In the game DeLappe drops his weapon and starts typing the names of all the American soldiers who died during the Iraq war. The performance ended on December 18, 2011, the announced withdrawal date of the last U.S. troops in Iraq. Delappe had entered a total of 4484 names in the game.

These anti-war performances often get strong reactions from other players. The poems and the name of the killed soldiers remind the players about the reality of war, which make them angry and uncomfortable. The players ask DeLappe to stop what he's doing, but when he continues they shoot him or simply kick him out of the game. You can see the strong reactions from the other players as a proof that DeLappe's performances are successful. He succeeds to break the game illusion, in the same way as Brecht "Verfremdungseffekt" breaks the illusion in drama. Brecht wrote that the distancing effect (Verfremdungseffekt) "prevents the audience from losing itself passively and completely in the character created by the actor, and which consequently leads the audience to be a consciously critical observer." [4] Or, in DeLappe's words:

> I see these works as a way to break through and perhaps expand the notion of "the magic circle" in gaming. We do not 'play' in contexts that are unrelated to our political, social and economic realities. Reactions during the first performance, *Howl* were mostly humorous. I recall one player noting "wow, poetry and shooting!". Reactions to my work have been most fierce within the context of the ongoing project, *dead-in-iraq*, commenced in 2006. Other players routinely insult me, demand to know why I am doing what I am doing and are generally very hostile. [5]

I'd like to mention two more performances by DeLappe: *Quake / Friends* and *ET tu?, Alfred*. *Quake / Friends* took place on October 18, 2002 and consisted of six people linked up online at the same venue in the game Quake III. In the game they began to perform an entire episode from the series Friends. Each participant played a character in the series and then wrote up his lines in the text field that is used by players in the game to communicate with each other. Since Quake is a game about killing as many opponents as possible to win, the performance was constantly interrupted when one of the participants was killed by the other players and was then forced to re-emerge to continue the performance.

The performance was mentioned in an article in the *New York Times*, followed by a cease and desist letter from Warner Bros., which owns the rights of the series, to DeLappe. In a settlement DeLappe refrained from carrying out the plans for a *Quake / Friends 2* performance. Instead, he staged his *Quake / Friends* performance again on March 8, 2003. This time the performance was made live in an art gallery. At six computers sat the participants logged into Quake, and their screens were projected on the gallery wall so anyone who was in the gallery could follow the performance live.

ET tu?, Alfred was premiered in November 2003 and was played out in the computer game Aliens Vs. Predator. In this case, the dialogue was taken from Spielberg's film *ET: the Extra Terrestrial* and mixed with statements made by the Iranian Merhan Karimi Nasseri (Sir Alfred), who for 15 years lived as an illegal refugee in the Paris airport. In 2004, Spielberg made *The Terminal*, based on the story of Karimi Nasseri. Both the alien ET and Sir Alfred are in a sense stranded refugees who are trying to find a home, and this is the subject of DeLappe's performance.

Eva and Franco Mattes aka 0100101110101101.org

In 2003, Linden Labs started the online world Second Life (SL) which gave artists new possibilities to create on-line performance. Second Life is a 3D virtual world with its own currency and economy. With your money you can buy land, build houses, organize art exhibitions: yes, in SL you can do anything you can do in real life, and more. The freedom to build and create your own world soon made SL an important platform for artistic experiments. In 2006 Second Front, one of the first performance groups in SL, was founded. Second Front consist today of seven members: Gazira Babeli, Yael Gilks, Bibbe Hansen, Doug Jarvis, Scott Kildall, Patrick Lichty and Liz Solo. You could probably write a whole book about Second Front and performance art in Second Life, but in this survey I chose to focus on another artist group working with performance in SL.

Eva and Franco Mattes aka 0100101110101101.org call their performance series *Synthetic Performances*:

Synthetic Performances are online live gaming sessions inside the virtual world of Second Life, performed by Eva and

Franco Mattes through their avatars, which were constructed from their bodies and faces. People can attend and interact with the live performances connecting to the video-game from all over the world. [6]

In 2007 they started to re-enact several important performances from the history of art: *Shoot* (1971), where the artist Chris Burden got shot with a rifle by a friend; Vito Acconci's *Seedbed* (1972), where the artist, hidden under a ramp in the Sonnabend Gallery in New York, masturbated while describing his fantasies about the visitors who walked on the ramp above him; and Valie Export and Peter Weibel's *Tap and Touch Cinema*, which took place in various locations in Europe in the late sixties.

Tap and Touch Cinema consisted of a box with a curtain that Valie Export wore in front of her naked torso. This portable cinema was a protest against the way women and sexuality were described in movies. The crowds on the street were invited to visit Valie's cinema putting their hands behind the curtain and feeling the "movie", that is her breasts. The audience was no longer a passive observer, but had to act and decide what "appeared" in Export's movie theatre.

Another re-created performance by the Mattes including nude bodies was Marina Abramović and Ulay's *Imponderabilia*, originally performed in 1977 in the Modern Art Museum in Bologna. In the original performance, the two artists stood naked on the main entrance of the museum. The visitors had to squeeze themselves between the two naked bodies to enter the exhibition.

Performances in SL and other on-line games are performed by avatars actors. An avatar is a graphic character representing the player in a virtual world. The above mentioned performances are originally about the body, and they are very tactile. The visitor is often confronted with a situation that might arouse discomfort: a man gets shot, someone is masturbating, an unknown woman offers the audience to feel her breasts, the visitor has to squeeze herself between two naked bodies. When these works are re-created in a virtual world, several important senses as smell and touch are missing. To see an avatar being shot, or to walk between two naked avatars is far from being the same experience you can have in real life. The Mattes' performances therefore arouse other questions: why are people acting differently in a virtual world and in real life? The original *Imponderabilia* and the Mattes' re-enactment are basically the same concept, the only difference being the setting. And yet, they provide a totally different experience.

The *Synthetic Performances* series was completed in 2007 with *7000 Oaks* (after Joseph Beuys) and *The Singing Sculpture* (after Gilbert and George). *7000 Oaks* was Beuys' contribution to Documenta 7 in 1982. With the help of volunteers Beuys started to plant 7000 oaks in the German city Kassel, each tree accompanied by a basalt stone. The project took 5 years to be completed. Twenty-five years later the Mattes made the same installation in SL: they started planting virtual trees and stack boulders on an island in SL, inviting other users to participate in the project. While the relational side of Beuys' performance is kept, its ecological side is completely lost. In *The Singing Sculpture* (1969), Gilbert & George – their faces covered with golden paint – stood on a table in the gallery, dancing and singing the traditional English song "Underneath the Arches". Almost forty years later, the Mattes' avatars did the same in a virtual space.

In 2009 Eva and Franco Mattes presented three new performances: *I know that it's all a state of mind*, *I can't find myself either* and *Medication Valse*. These performances are still about body and nudity, but the big difference is that the Mattes are now using the full repertoire that virtual worlds provide for avatar performances. In a virtual world you can change the physical rules by means of hacking and software manipulation, and allow your avatar to do things impossible for bodies in the real world: you can fly, assume unnatural positions without pain, fall into other avatars and walk into object that should be solid.

Rainey Straus and Katherine Isbister

In 2004, Rainey Straus and Katherine Isbister made a performance called *SimBee*, a parody of Vanessa Beecroft's installations recreated in the game The Sims. The Sims is a simulation game where players can create their own family and then let the family move into a house in a virtual community. The task is to ensure that all members of the family are happy and contented. One could compare The Sims to an advanced virtual dollhouse. Vanessa Beecroft, on the other hand, is an Italian artist who has worked with performance art in museums, where she makes use of scantily clad female models who pose in the exhibition space as a sort of living Barbie dolls. Beecroft works in the intersection of fashion and art, and often focuses on how we view people. In *SimBee* Straus and Isbister staged a Beecroft-style installation in a virtual gallery, but after a while the Sim models started to live their own life and the performance degenerated in a disastrous way with fires, fights and violence. In an interview Ibister explains why she and Straus choose to use a video game as The Sims for performance art:

Games invite our participation and projection – we are actors in these virtual spaces, and they are such plastic, malleable worlds. They are a tremendously powerful venue for exploring issues of representation, of identity, of control of our own image, as well as issues of aesthetics and how our senses are framed by the context in which we experience art. The Sims itself is a world in which these kinds of explorations are happening on a mass scale for everyday consumers, and was a ripe context for conducting such investigations. [7]

Caleb Larsen

Another artist that have been working with The Sims is the American artist Caleb Larsen. In Larsen's case it was not a re-enactment of a previous performance but a new one with himself in the leading role. Larsen reconstructed as far as it was possible with the Sims technology, elements of his life, family, apartment and neighborhood in the game. He also created an avatar, a virtual character with a life similar to his own. In June 2005 the performance, with the title *Simulacrum* was performed in the Tjaden Gallery at Cornell University. For one week Larsen acted as his virtual self from 9:00 am to 4:30 pm in the virtual world of The Sims. During the exhibition he maintained a weblog documenting his life by posting screenshots and captions from the game. On his homepage Larsen explains that the inspiration for *Simulacrum* came from artists such as Allan Kaprow and Tehching Hsieh. In the sixties Kaprow made happenings where the audience was invited to share experiences in which he had incorporated everyday activities. The American artist Tehching Hsieh also mixes art and real life. In his *One Year Performance* he lives for a year after fixed rules: for example, he is not allowed to go indoor, talk, make art etc. Larsen's *Simulacrum* is also a mix of art and life, but in this case it's a virtual life. The audience can participate in the artist's virtual life for a week.

Mark Beasley and Pippin Barr

As an artist you don't have to use existing video games or on-line worlds to re-create famous performances: you always have the possibility to create your own game. In 2007, American artist Mark Beasley made *Vito Acconci (The video game)*, a suite of three new video games in which the player can re-enact famous performances by Acconci: *Seedbed*, *Center* and *Following Piece*. In these games, it's the player, and not the artist, who re-enacts the performances with the help of a Wii remote control. In *Following Piece*, for example, Acconci selected randomly a person he met on the street, and started to stalk her until she entered a private place. In Beasley's game your goal is to stalk a person on the street, but if the distance to the person is too long you loose the game and have to start all over again.

In the video game *The Artist Is Present* Pippin Barr re-created a recent performance by Marina Abramović, staged at the Museum of Modern Art in New York in 2010. As in Beasley's games, the graphic is simple and reminds of the early 2D 8-bit games from the eighties. In Abramović performance, people are allowed to sit for a couple of minutes in front of the artist and watch into her eyes. The performance evolved in a big media event, with many people – including vips – queuing for hours to meet the artist. The game is therefore basically about waiting: waiting for the museum to open, waiting in the queue to meet the artist eye to eye. Waiting is an essential part of our life – as Samuel Beckett showed in his drama *Waiting for Godot* – but it's an unusual experience in games. As Barr explains [8]:

> Waiting is such a no-no in games [...] it's regarded as so abusive, and yet it's a major part of life. To the extent we want games to (sometimes) be "about life", waiting is fair game.

Conclusion

Since the sixties performance artist have tried to explore and find new groups and arenas outside the established art institutions. With the development of the internet and on-line worlds artists started to use avatars actors to create performances and meet a new public from all around the world. Joseph Delappe tries to establish a dialogue with the gamers by interfering and breaking the illusion in the game. Eva and Franco Mattes and others re-enact classic works from the sixties in digital environments. An essential part of real-life performances is to explore the body, the conventions and the taboos associated with social relationships. Most of these classic performances re-enacted today in on-line worlds are tactical and try to affect or shock the visitor. But in the virtual world there is another set of rules and we behave in different ways because we know this is only fiction. You can shoot people, go around naked and do other things that are not accepted in the real world without shocking people. These new contexts make the performances get a new meaning when restaged in on-line worlds. Instead of breaking the rules of human behavior, many of these performances want to break the rules of the game. DeLappe breaks the players' illusion by reminding them that there is a real war outside the virtual world. Pippin Barr introduce the dimensions of waiting and boredom, always banned from games. If real life performance is mainly about our bodies, on-line performance is more about breaking the illusion and the rules of the virtual environment, to make us aware that we are in an artificial world.

First published in *Hz-Journal #17*, April 2012.

[1] Cf. http://en.wikipedia.org/wiki/Performance_art.
[2] Mathias Jansson, "Antoinette LaFarge's Mixed Realities", in *Gamescenes.org*, October 2011.
[3] Mathias Jansson, "Joseph Delappe, pioneer of online game performance art", in *Gamescenens.org*, May 2005.
[4] John Willett (ed.), *Brecht on Theatre*, New York: Hill and Wang, 1964, p. 91.
[5] Mathias Jansson, "Joseph Delappe, pioneer of online game performance art", cit.
[6] Cf. www.0100101110101101.org/.
[7] Mathias Jansson, "Katherine Isbister and the Art of The Sims", in *Gamescenes.org*, December 2010.
[8] Mathias Jansson, "Interview with Pippin Barr – The Artist is Present", in *Next-Level*, September 2011.

Pain Is Not the Game: Virtual and Real in Video Game Art

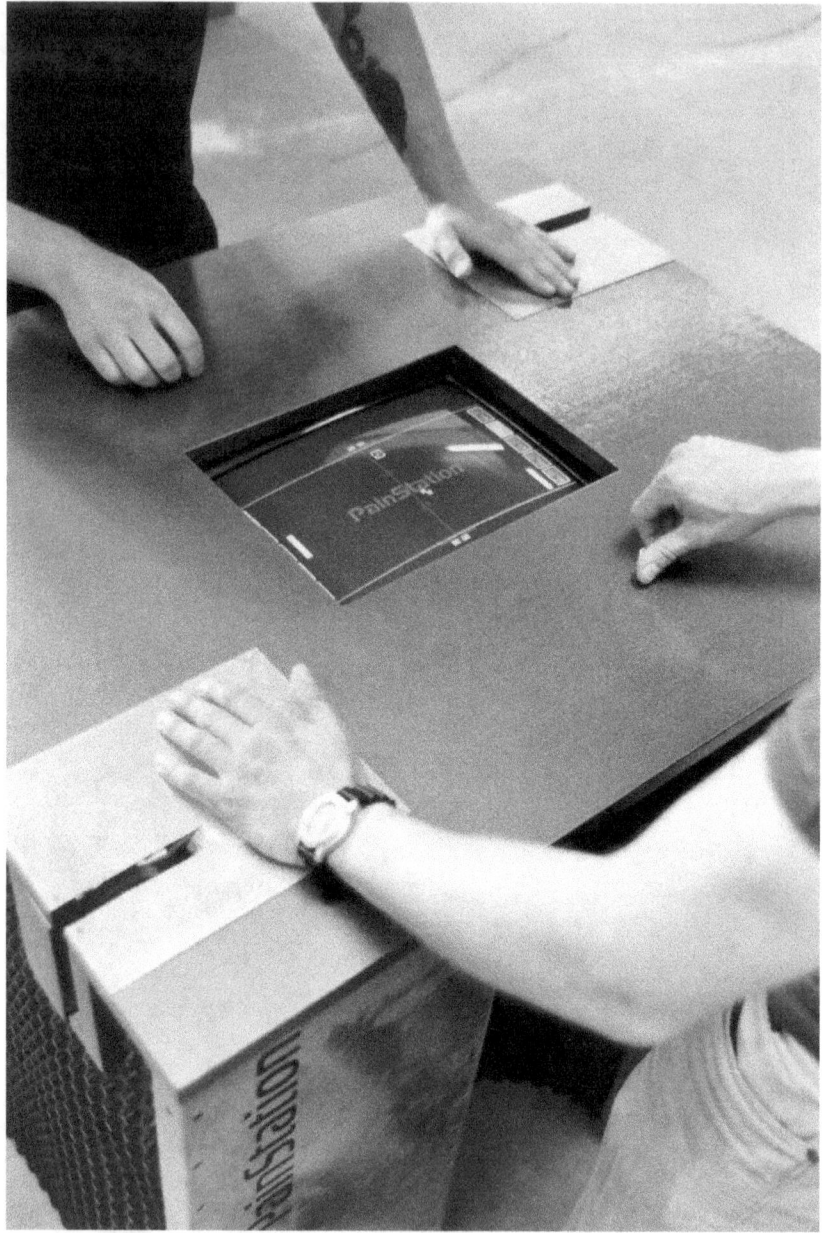

Volker Morawe, Tilman Reiff, *PainStation*, 2001 - 2004. Installation view at the O.K Center for Contemporary Art Upper Austria, during Ars Electronica 2002. Image courtesy O.K Center

When German artists Volker Morawe and Tilman Reiff were young, they used to play games that deal with punishment in some ways. Reiff explains:

> The most popular was probably Folter-Mau-Mau: a simple card game where the looser would be punished according to the cards that remain in his hand. We remember the special tension that arose from the threat of possible punishment and the excitement that came with it. The relief if you came away unpunished. It simply adds a lot of feelings to the experience.

Today we spend a lot of our time playing games in virtual worlds. Compared with the games Reiff and Morawe used to play, the graphical development has been enormous. Today, video games have photorealistic high definition graphics, but still virtual game worlds miss some important experiences compared to a simple cardgame as Folter-Mau-Mau.

You can be beaten, kicked, stabbed, hit, shoot, drive off a cliff, jump from a skyscraper or be blown to pieces, but whatever happens on the screen you don't feel any physical pain in your body, because it's only a game. The lack of physical experience in video games becomes quite obvious when you attend one of Eva and Franco Mattes' re-enactments in Second Life. The Mattes have re-enacted some classic performances, such as Chris Burden's *Shoot*, Valie Export and Peter Weibel's *Tapp und Tastkino* and Marina Abramović and Ulay's *Imponderabilia*. In these re-enactments, several aspects of the original performance such as odour, heat, friction, facial expressions, and other bodily experiences are missing: they get lost in the translation from reality to virtuality.

To see a graphic avatar get shot as in the re-enactment of Burden's *Shoot* (1971) is something else than to be in the gallery and see the bullet hit the flesh of a real human. Also, it's a bit different to take a bullet in real life and in a virtual world. I'm sure Chris Burden would agree with me, but this is also what the Mattes' performance puts its finger on. The virtual world is a safe zone, you can do and be anything you like, because there is no physical danger threatening your body. You can of course get a mouse arm or a stiff neck if you play video games to long, but that's something else which is connected to what you are doing in the real world, not in the virtual.

Since the video game industry is struggling towards a total immersion, there are of course many game designer and artists that have tried to re-create the missing sensations that get lost in the translation. Today we have the Xbox 360 kinect capture technique, the Wii consoles and forced feeback controls and of course the Cave and VR-technique, which are expensive installations where the visitor with help of special glasses and gloves can move and interact in a virtual room, but still there are many human senses that are missing in the virtual worlds. Pain for example.

In 2000, Eddo Stern and Mark Allen did a performance called *Tekken Torture Tournament*. Tekken is a martial art game, in which you should kick and hit your opponent until he is defeated. In the performance the participating players were equipped with special bracelets. When the player was hit by the other player on the screen he got an electric shock in the arm. The more hits the opponents got the more pain the second player had to suffer. The bracelet was a form of interface that could connect the virtual pain with the player's psychical body and transfer the virtual violence into the real world.

Another example of an art work that is transferring pain from the virtual world into the real is the game *Painstation*. The German collective ///////fur/// (Volker Morawe, Tilman Reiff and Roman Kirschner) has developed a game cabinet which is basically a simple PONG game. When you miss the ball the opponent uses to win a point, but in this version the loser is also punished by an electric shock, heat or a whiplash on his hand. The virtual defeat is transformed into real pain, as in *Tekken Torture Tournament*. The player that cannot stand the pain and removes his hand loses the game. Reiff explains:

> The group met at the Academy of Media Arts Cologne. It was during our studies – we moved in together and had a shared office in our apartment. One year later – in 2001 – the *Painstation* was born and we founded /////////fur//// as a label for our collaborative work. *Painstation* is based on the idea to incorporate the body into the gaming experience, to make gaming a more physical experience.

In Riley Hamond's installation *What it is without the hand that wields it* (2008) you could also find the discussion about the physical experience of gaming. The installation was an electronic sculpture attached to a server where people played Counterstrike. The sculpture consisted of a number of blood bags with tubing that was connected to nozzles, that were opened when one of the players on the server was shoot. The virtual killing and violence ran so to speak over to reality, the virtual blood in the game was solidified on the gallery floor.

In Hamond's work it's not the pain that is transferred but instead body fluids: virtual blood is leaking out from the server and is transformed into "real" blood on the gallery floor. Again, it's a bit different to see blood in a video game or in a film and stand in front of it – even strong guys use to faint in the sight of real blood bleeding from bodies.

The big difference between what we experience and feel in virtual worlds and in the real world is also something that could affect our behaviour. The virtual world is a fantasy and we are not physically affected in any way by our actions so we are doing things we usually shouldn't do as killing people, driving too fast, jumping from skyscrapers etc. But what happens when the boundaries between virtuality and reality are not so clear and fixed? In Wafaa Bilal's installation *Domestic Tension* these questions are in focus. During a month in 2007 Bilal lived in the Flat File Gallery in Chicago, constantly monitored by a webcam, and constantly threatened by a paintball gun that anyone via a website could fire at him. To fire a paintball gun from a website with your mouse is not so different from shooting in video games: it's only a click on the mouse. The consequences are, of course, very different, since you are shooting a man of flesh and blood, not a digital object. And yet, even if aware of this situation, a lot of people were willing to shoot Bilal. On the computer screen the visitors could see a silent, black and white image from the surveillance camera with the rigged paintball gun, which meant that many important senses were lost in the communication between the gallery and the viewer. If the visitor had to go to the gallery, pick up the paintball gun and fire the gun when he stood eye to eye with his victim, he would probably have behaved differently and reflect on the situation.

As in the case of Eva and Franco Mattes' performances, the missing physical feelings and senses make us behave differently when we experience a virtual performance compared with a real one.

Virtual art is today very common, so the challenge is no longer to transform reality into virtuality, but to recreate the feelings and experience of reality that are missing in the virtual world. It will probably take some years before we could experience the science fiction dream of a total immersion portrayed by movies like *The Matrix* and surrogates. Tilman Reiff believes that, at some point, we'll have a Startrek holodeck in our living room and play video games as in "reality"; until then, we have to be satisfied to feel the pain in the game.

First published in *Digimag*, Issue 60, December 2010.

Video Game Appropriation in Contemporary Art

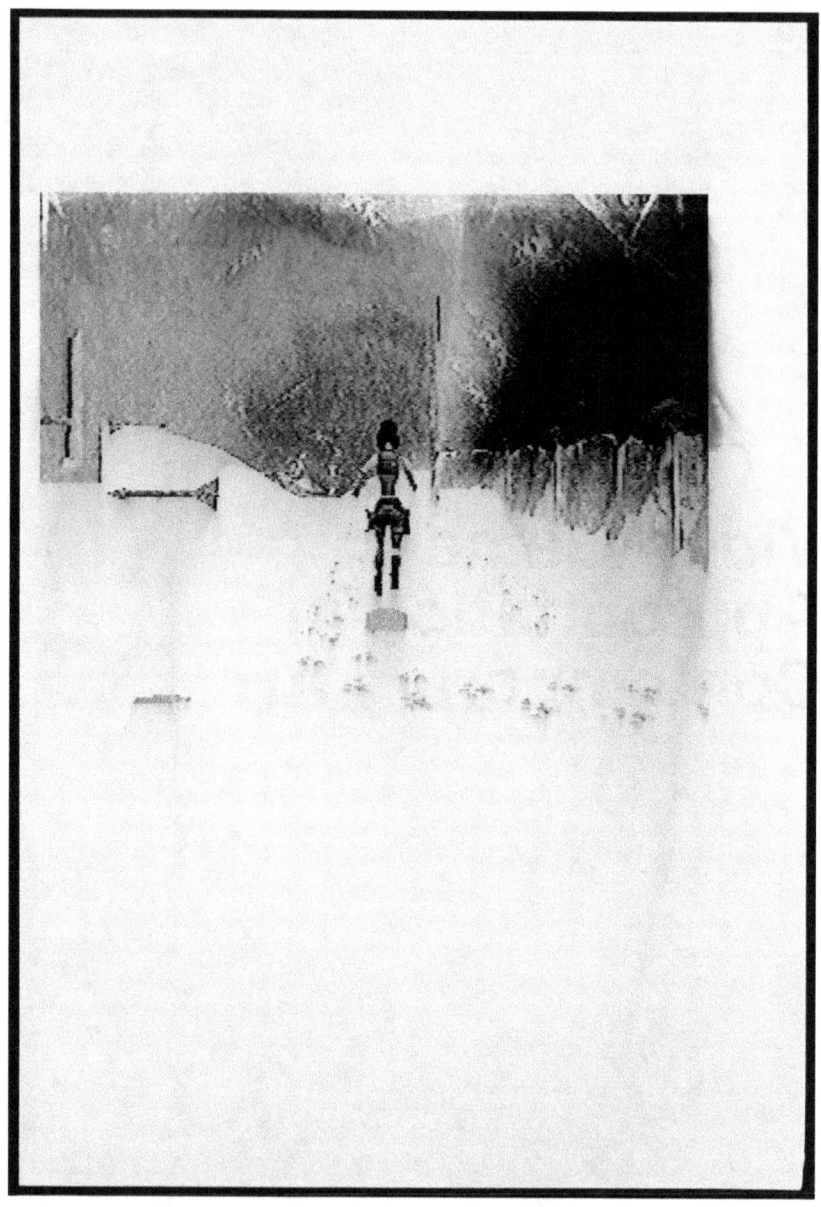

Miltos Manetas, *after TombRaider #2*, 1996. Vibracolour print on superglossy paper, 50x75 inches. Edition: unique. Image courtesy the artist

Appropriation is a fundamental aspect in the history of the arts (literary, visual, musical). Appropriation can be understood as "the use of borrowed elements in the creation of a new work." In the visual arts, to appropriate means to properly adopt, borrow, recycle or sample aspects (or the entire form) of man-made visual culture. [1]

Artists have always borrowed and used elements, symbols and characters both from art history and popular culture. Marcel Duchamp's *Mona Lisa* with a mustache is a classic example of appropriation in art. Andy Warhol's *Campbell Soup*, Roy Lichtenstein paintings which look like old fashioned comic strips, Dara Birnbaum's video art based on the TV-series *Wonder Woman* and Richard Prince's photographs of the Marlboro man's commercials are other art works that are often highlighted as examples of appropriation in contemporary art.

Classic video games such as Pong, Tetris, Space Invaders, Pac Man and Super Mario have also in the past decade inspired many artists to create new works of art. The common link between all of these games is that they are very easy to learn and play. There is no need for manuals, just a few simple instructions on the screen. The graphics are simple, the colors a few, the characters and style are pixelated. These games have influenced a whole generation and over time have become a part of our cultural heritage. Even today, these games still amuse and fascinate players and inspire artists to use them in their art. There are of course other examples with more modern games as The Sims, Tomb Raider, racing games and First Person Shooters.

In this essay, we will take a closer look at some of these games and give examples of how they have been used by artists in different ways to make art, in the attempt to show the impact they had on the art scene.

Pong

It was the American physicist William Higinbotham who in 1958 created what many consider to be the first computer game. The game was called Tennis for Two and was played on an oscilloscope with the help of a simple analogue control. However, only in 1972 the game became one of the first real big sellers for the computer games industry. That year the Atari Company, founded by Allan Alcorn and Nolan Bushnell, picked up the idea and created a commercial version called PONG.

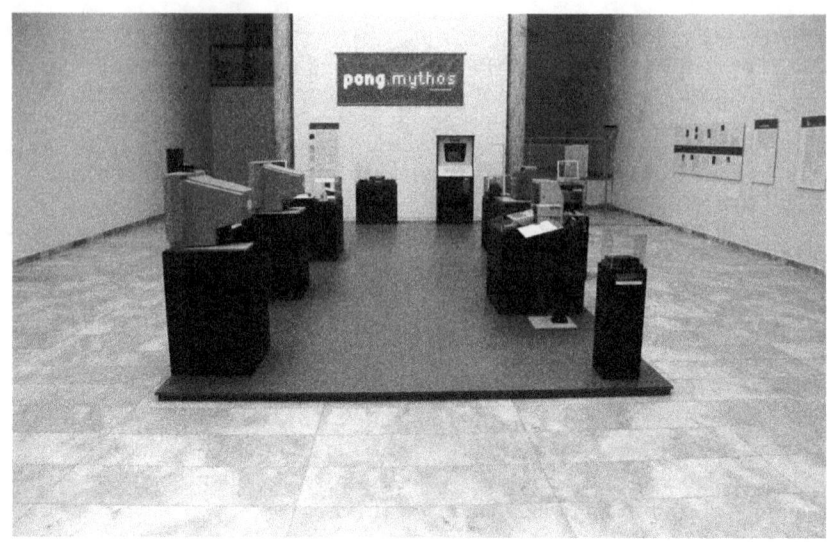

The exhibition "pong.mythos" installed at the Kunstverein Stuttgart (february 11 – March 19, 2006). Photo: Mathilde Mupe

PONG is a simple, minimalistic game that consists of two rectangles and a square, which symbolize two tennis racquets and a ball. You can either play against another opponent or against the computer. In this simplified version of tennis, the goal is to hit the ball so the opponent misses it.

PONG is probably the video game that has inspired most artists over the past decade. When, in 2007, the Computer Games Museum in Berlin organized a major exhibition entitled "pong.mythos", over 30 artists were included with works of art inspired by PONG. The catalogue explains why PONG fascinated so many artists:

> No other video game has been the origin of artistic production quite as often as the simple black-and-white tennis game. In addition to its popularity, it seems to be this minimalism that especially appeals to artists, since the playing pattern is a virtual prototype of the essence of each and every communication situation: the ball as the smallest possible unit of information, oscillating between sender and receiver. [2]

The artist group ////////fur//// showed their *Pain Station* (2001) in which the players who missed the ball were punished with physical pain, a blow on the hand, heat or an electric shock. *Pain Station* connects the physical world with the virtual and the virtual player's mistakes turn into real pain.

The artist group Blinkenlights was represented with a project that transformed a large office building in Berlin's Alexanderplatz into a digital screen where passersby could play PONG on the facade with the help of their mobile phones. In Sebastian Hanig and Gordan Savicic's work *BioPong* (2005) the ball was replaced with a living cockroach where the players would try to push the insect over to the other side. And in the group Time's Up version *Sonic Body Pong* (2006) the ball in the game was experienced by the players purely through sound. They hear a spatially accurate soundscape which is determined by both the orientation of their heads and their position on the court, and they must determine where to move their body based on the sound of the approaching ball.

There are many other examples that were not included in the exhibition "pong.mythos". As early as 1999, Natalie Bookchin made *The Intruder*, a work where PONG was one of 10 different video games that she used to turn Jorge Louis Borges' short story *The Intruder* into an interactive artwork. Danish artist Anders Visti mixed the game PONG with the art of Piet Mondrian in *PONGdrian v1.0* (2007). The playing field in Visti's artwork is reminiscent of a painting by Mondrian but when the ball hits something, it disturbs the lines and color fields, and introduces new opportunities and challenges for the player. Finally, Swiss artist Guillaume Reymond has made a series of performances called *Game Over*. In a theater auditorium, he generates animated sequences by using real people in colorful T-shirts, where each individual represents a square on a screen. By moving the people in the auditorium, he can create short video sequences, some inspired by PONG's minimal graphics.

Why is PONG so popular among artists? It is one of the very first video games, and therefore there is a large identification factor and a strong relationships between the game, the player and the artwork. Being one of the easiest games both in terms of appearance and learning, it's also easy to transform it and use it in different contexts. The Modernist dogma "less is more" may thus be a good way to explain why PONG has inspired so many artists in recent years.

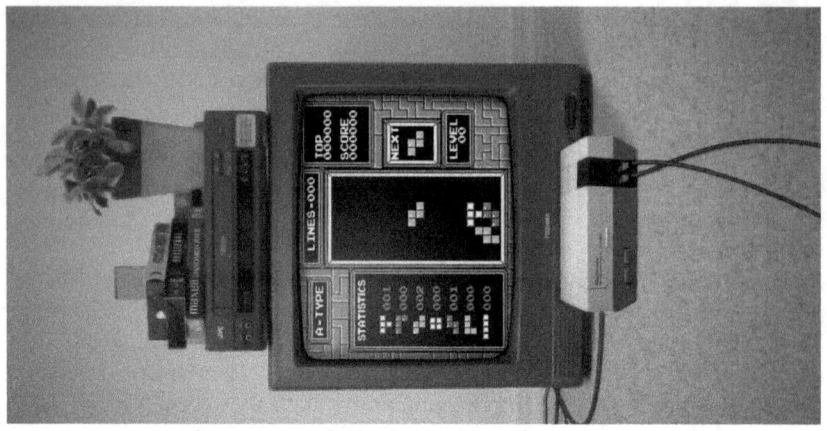

David Kraftsow, *First Person Tetris*, 2010. Screenshot

Tetris

Made in 1984 and officially released in 1985 by the Russian programmer Alexey Pajitnov, Tetris is a game that the Cubists would have worshipped. To play, you have to move and rotate seven different combinations of blocks as they fall into a well. The blocks are called tetrominos and are made of four squares. The goal is to fit the different geometric shapes so that as little empty space as possible remains in the bottom of the well. Tetris is a puzzle game for people who like compact living, and who see it as a sport to pack economically to the holiday.

Contemporary artists approached Tetris in at least three different ways. The Swedish artist Michael Johansson is a good example of the first approach. He has used the basic idea of Tetris to stack objects with different colors and shape. Johansson works with site-specific installations, in which he collects and stacks objects from the near surroundings in perfect symmetry, with no spaces in between them. The installations are called Tetris, which is fitting since they are strongly reminiscent of the game. Johansson says in an interview for *Gamescenes.org*:

> For me creating works by stacking and organizing ordinary objects is very much about putting things we all recognize from a certain situation into a new context, and by this altering their meaning. And I think for me the most fascinating thing

with the Tetris-effect is the fusion of two different worlds, that something you recognize from the world of the video game merges into the real life as well, and makes you step out from your daily routine and look at things in a different way. [3]

Like many other classical video games, Tetris has been used a lot in in graffiti, mosaics and posters installed in public spaces. In 2008, Ella Barclay, Adrianne Tasker, Ben Backhouse and Kelly Robson for an exhibition at Gaffa Gallery in Sydney, Australia, designed an installation where they placed giant illuminated Tetris blocks in a narrow alley. It looked exactly as if the blocks had fallen from the sky, but the alley had been too narrow so the blocks were stuck halfway down.

The second approach is to move Tetris out from the exhibition room into public spaces and sometimes also create interactive and social art. The artist group Blinkenlights, known for transforming large skyscrapers into interactive screens, made it possible for the passers-by to play Pong or Tetris on a skyscraper using a mobile phone. In 2002 they made the installation *Arcade*, which turned one of the skyscrapers of the Bibliotheque Nationale de France in Paris into a giant screen showing various animations.

In early 2010 the Spanish artist group Lummo (Carles Gutierrez, Javier Lloret, Mar Canet & Jordi Puig) installed a Tetris game in which four people have to cooperate to play it. The first step for the participations was to create the Tetris blocks and after that they had to work together to place them in the right position in the well projected on a wall. Both Blinkenlights and Lummo are creating public meeting places with social interaction where the video game is used as an interface.

The third approach is changing the game itself and creates new versions of it, discussing the game concept itself. *1d Tetris*, by zigah, is a one-dimensional Tetris where the blocks consist of four vertical squares falling into a well that is just one block wide. Since the blocks always fill the well the players do not have to do anything to score points. The basic idea of the falling blocks still remains in the game, but in a one-dimensional world there is no longer any difficulty, the game is reduced to a very monotonous and predictable puzzle game.

In *First Person Tetris*, David Kraftsow combines the first person shooter perspective with the ordinary puzzle game. In Kraftsow's variant you see the game from a first person perspective so when you spin the blocks, it's not the individual blocks that are spinning around but the whole screen. Just by using a new perspective, Kraftsow created a whole new experience of Tetris.

Mauro Ceolin has spent many years focusing on the modern emblems of the Internet. In works such as *RGBTetris* and *RGBInvaders* he replaces the game's graphics with contemporary icons and logos. In *RGBTetris* the blocks that fall down the well turned into logos of Camel, McDonalds, Nike and Mercedes.

The most interesting and most independent among the playable Tetris versions that I have found are made by the Swedish artist Ida Roden. In *Composition Grid* she has combined her interest in drawing with Tetris. The player can play a game and in the same time create a unique drawing by rotating and changing one of the 216 different creatures that Roden has created, with the Tetris blocks as model. The player can then choose to print out their own game plan with the artist's signature, and in that way have a unique work of art in there possession.

Tetris, this two-dimensional version of Rubik's Cube, seems to provide a lot of room for artistic experimentation. It just needs some simple changes, or new perspectives, to create new and interesting interpretations of the game.

Super Mario

The Italian plumber Mario appeared for the first time in 1981 as a character in the video game Donkey Kong, created by the famous Japanese game developer Shigeru Miyamoto. Two years later, Mario became the main character of his own game, and his fame grew exponentially. Since then, approximately 200 different video games have been produced where Mario has the leading role.

The artist who has done the most famous works based on the video game is Cory Arcangel, whose iconic work *Super Mario Clouds* got the cover of Artforum and is now in the permanent collection of the Whitney Museum, New York. Made in 2002, it was exhibited at the Whitney Biennial in 2004. In *Super Mario Clouds* Arcangel has hacked and changed an old Nintendo game cartridge so that the only thing that remains of the original game are the little white fluffy clouds that slowly scroll by on a clear blue sky. Since Arcangel has taken away all of the game elements and interaction, you can refer to it as an anti-game. You can also interpret the work as a renewal and a commentary on the art historical genre of cloud painting that became popular during the 1800s, when the science of cloud formations and their appearance emerged.

Super Mario Movie is a 15 minute video made with Paper Rad in 2005. Again, it is a hacked Nintendo cartridge, and in the opening scene you can read the following text: "As a video game grows old its content and internal logic deteriorate. For a character caught in this breakdown problems affect every area of life." For Mario, it means that when his world grows older its graphic content and logic breaks down until he finds himself trapped into a nightmare where he falls head over heels down the screen in an evolving fragmented world of psychedelic colours in which, among other things, a giant Mario head pops up. What Arcangel describes is the natural degradation process that eventually affects all physical storage devices from floppy disks and CDs to hard drives. When the stored information gets corrupted by aging it results into misreading with strange and illogical effects on the screen. It's not just we human that are having problems when our cells and DNA are getting old, game characters can experience strange behaviours and diseases when their data age as well.

In the video *Naptime* (2002) we find Mario sleeping in his bed. Above him, a dream cloud features a psychedelic stream of characters and colours – the same effect you can experience when you try to run old games that have become damaged or when you are using a computer with a broken graphic card. Just like in *Super Mario Movie*, in *Naptime* a nightmare is chasing Mario again. It is a world of corrupted code and information in which the game logic has broken down, a world that behaves as if it was infected by a nasty computer virus.

Artist Miltos Manetas has also created a video with a sleeping Mario. In the three-minute long *Super Mario Sleeping* (1987) we see how Mario gets tired and lies down and sleeps in the grass. Just like in Arcangel's work, we are confronted with an anti-game: all the interactivity and stress in the game are removed, and we experience a calm and meditative atmosphere. Philip K. Dick novel *Do Androids Dream of Electric Sheep?* (1968) comes into mind. What is it that distinguishes a human from an android or a character in a video game? Can characters in computer games dream and, in that case, what are they dreaming of when we are not playing them?

It's not just the Mario character that is interesting for artists, but also the objects in the game. Australian artist Antoinette J. Citizen created in 2008 the interactive installation *Super Mario Brothers Level 1-1* in which she transformed an art gallery into a Super Mario game. She painted the walls with different levels of the game and installed interactive boxes with question marks and bricks. The visitor could touch the boxes which then produced different sounds from the game. Citizen's works are, like many other Game Art works, an example of how artists transfer the virtual game world into the real exhibition space.

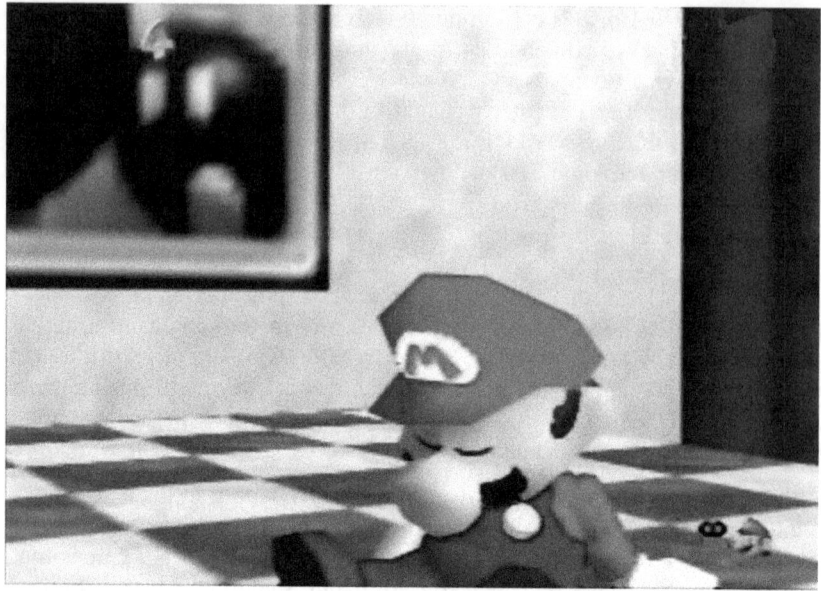

Miltos Manetas, *Supermario Sleeping*, 1998. Dvd after SuperMario for Nintendo 64. Courtesy the artist.

Mario is probably the most famous character in the video game world. Is he maybe as famous as Jesus? The Polish artist Kordian Lewandowski plays with this idea in the work *Game Over*. He has created a copy of Michelangelo's famous *Pietà* sculpture but instead of a dying Christ in the arms of the Virgin Mary, we see Mario lying lifeless in the arms of Princess Peach. With their own iconography and stories about the constant struggle between good and evil, at some degree, video games seem to have taken over the role of religion.

Space Invaders

Tomohiro Nishikado's classic video game Space Invaders (1978) can be seen as a metaphor for the Cold War and the fears for an approaching nuclear war. An extraterrestrial army is marching closer to Earth. Only a lone cannon stands between the intergalactic monsters and the complete annihilation of mankind. The lonely hero struggling against evil is a theme that we recognise from myths, films and books. With its clear and pedagogical symbolic language, Space Invaders has inspired several contemporary artists to describe the eternal struggle between good and evil in our time.

In British artists Thomson & Craighead's *Triggerhappy* (1998), the aliens are replaced with quotes taken from French philosopher Michael Foucault's essay "What is an author?". *Triggerhappy* is a work that explores the relationship between hyper-text, author and reader. What is a writer, or rather, who is the artist when we are dealing with interactive art in the form of a video game? Is it Tomohiro Nishikado, who created the original game? Is it Thomson & Craighead, who have modified it? Is it the player, who is playing the game? Or is it the computer, that creates and interprets the text (the code) that makes the game appear on the screen?

After September 11, the world suddenly saw a new major enemy, international terrorism. In a modernized version of Space Invaders, Douglas Edric Stanley re-located the game into the Twin Towers in New York. In *Invaders!* (2008) you have to fight against the hostile aliens before they completely destroy the two towers. The classic struggle between good and evil continues: the game concept is the same as in the original, but the scenario and the metaphoric meaning of the aliens has changed.

The struggle between good and evil can also be found in other areas of our society, for example in class and gender struggle. In 2010, South African photojournalist Nadine Hutton made the game *Skirt-Invaders*. The main character in the game is Jacob Zuma, South African president since 2009. Zuma has been quite controversial because he is a polygamist and has expressed his doubts about the dangers of AIDS. In the game you have to shoot down a never-ending stream of virgins from the Zulu tribe. Will the president succeed to shoot down any threatening scandals before they land on the ground? Hutton's work is an example of how a well-known video game can be used for political purposes and be both entertaining and very critical at the same time.

The term mash-up, frequently used today, describes a form of digital collage. Ryan Snieder has made mash-ups by combining images from various sources, including Life magazine and video games. *Duck Hunt / Space Invader* shows a bird hunter with a dog, but it's not birds the hunter aims for, but Space Invaders. Those who played video games in the 70s and 80s will probably remember the game Duck Hunt, where you could shoot ducks that flew up out of the reeds. Snieder has combined the two game ideas. The work discusses the boundaries between real and digital. What happens when these two worlds become more integrated and their borders get increasingly blurred?

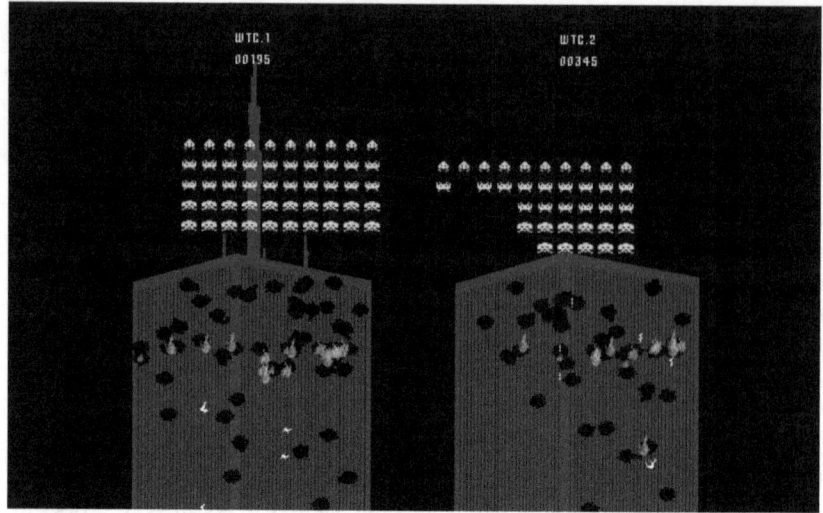

Douglas Edric Stanley, *Invaders!*, 2008. Screenshot, courtesy the artist.

We can't end up this short review without mentioning the French street artist who hides behind the pseudonym Space Invader. His main art project consists of "invading" various cities around the world and putting up small mosaics of characters from 8bit video games in public spaces. For each successful invasion, he collects points, and the whole art project is described on his website as a reality game. Like other forms of street art Space Invader is an ongoing battle about the public space. With help of popular culture Space Invader tries to infiltrate the commercial forces that control the imagery that appears in our public spaces. The aliens, in the form of small mosaics, become a force that can not be defeated when they are spreading all over the world. An important part of the game Space Invaders is that you cannot win, you can certainly come to the high score list, but you can never defeat the aliens, they are instead coming in faster and faster each time they are shot down. It's obviously a dystopian world view, but if we look at it from artist Space Invader's point of view, it's rather something positive. Art is a force that won't be stopped. The invasion has just begun and the struggle between good and evil continues...

Pac-Man

The legend says it was when the Japanese game developer Toru Iwatani took a slice of his pizza that the yellow game character known as Pac-Man made his appearance. In Pac-Man, we find a restless character hunting around in life's mazes, constantly seeking for pills to satisfy his insatiable desire. Meanwhile, the ghosts of anxiety are tracking him down.

What many players don't realize is that the game also contains an unanswered existential question. Where Pac-Man actually is in the short period of time when he escapes into the left or right end of the maze to pop up again on the other side of the maze? In Martina Kellner's work *Pac-Man Time Out*, shown at the exhibition *A MAZE* in Berlin in 2009, the artist made short video clips investigating what Pac-Man actually does when he is away from the monitor. In one clip, we find him at the airport queue with Ms. Pac-Man, ready to board. Are they planning to take a holiday away from the busy video game environment?

One thing is for sure: Pac-Man does no appear in contemporary art as much as his colleagues from other classic games such as Space Invaders and Super Mario. Yet, like many 8-bit characters, Pac-Man is well represented in street art and design. For example, the American street artist Katie Sokoler staged a real Pac-Man game in her quarters. But it is quite unusual to find installations, machinima or Art Games where Pac-Man has the leading role. This is a bit odd considering how famous Pac-Man is among the general public. French artist François Escuillie has even created a paleontological reconstruction of Pac-Man's skull, and in his work *Confessions of a Color-Eater*, the Swedish Johan Löfgren introduced the colour "Ms. Pac-Man-yellow". But despite this there are only a few interactive artworks based on Pac-Man.

Two exceptions are worth highlighting: *Pac-Mondrian* and *Eggregore*. *Pac-Mondrian* was created in its first version in 2002 by the Canadian artist group Price Budgets Boys and is described as a mix of Piet Mondrian, Pac-Man and Boggie Woogie music. The board consists of Piet Mondrian's painting *Broadway Boogie Woogie* (1942-43), inspired by Manhattan's street grid and boogie woogie music. The gameplay is the same of the original Pac-Man , but the the maze looks like Mondrian's painting. The game had three sequels: *Detroit Techno* (2005), *Tokyo Techno* (2006) and *Toronto Techno* (2006). There, the labyrinths are designed according to the stylized street grid of each city, executed in Mondrian's signature style. There is a similarity between *Pac-Mondrian* and Danish artist Anders Visti's work *PONGdrian v1.0*, in which Visti combines PONG with Mondrian's paintings.

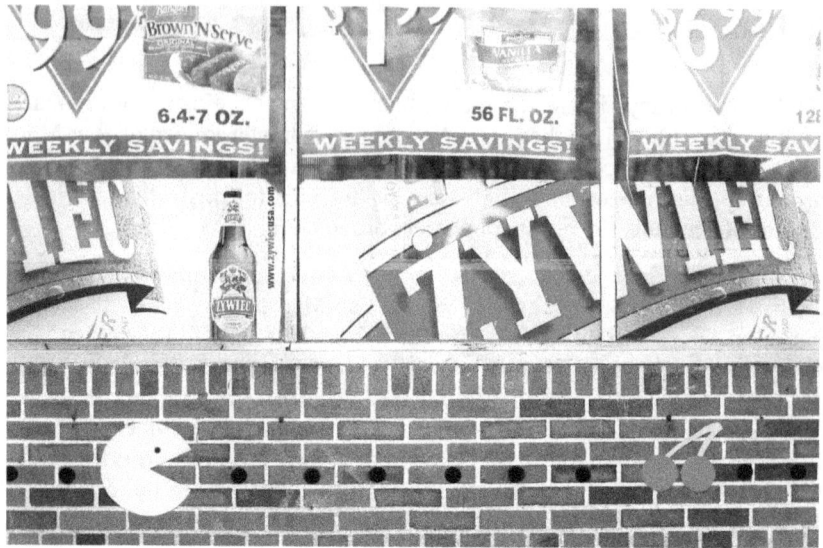

Katie Sokoler, *Real Life Pacman*, 2010. Image courtesy the artist.

Antonin Fourneau & Manuel Braun's work *Eggregor8* is a social video game in which eight players, each with its own control, try to collaborate and steer Pac-Man through the maze. It may sound like an old teamwork workshop with a twist. Eight wills and strategies must collaborate to succeed. "Eggregore" is a Greek word which is associated with occultism and represents a collective mind. The question that Fourneau and Braun are asking is: can multiple individual game strategies together create a stronger and better collective player, or will it just be chaos when the different games strategies are pulling in different directions? In the video game world, there are many examples of online worlds like World of Warcraft, where players successfully work together in clans or guilds in order to achieve higher goals in the game. It has even become an asset in your CV to show that you have played World of Warcraft and that you can lead and work together with other players to achieve different goals. Pac-Man, however, seems to be a rather greedy individualist who only thinks of himself. And perhaps it is this self-absorption that prevents the game from breaking through as a major theme in contemporary Game Art?

Racing Games

Pole Position, Outrun, F1 Racer and Need for Speed are some of the countless racing games that have attracted artists to explore a world of speed and burning rubber. In 2004 Cory Arcangel hacked the old Japanese Famicom driving game F1 Racer and removed, in the same way as he did in *Super Mario Clouds*, cars and other objects so that the only thing that remained of the game was the road and the landscape rushing toward the viewer.

If Arcangel employs hacking and game modification, other artists transfer virtual objects in the real world. In the exhibition *Objects of virtual desire* (2005), Swedish artists Simon Goldin and Jakob Senneby introduced virtual objects designed by gamers in Second Life. The objects were reproduced as limited edition art objects, exploring immaterial production in a virtual world and how it can be transferred into an economy of material production:

> *Objects of Virtual Desire* exploits the augmented value of immaterial objects to create and market tangible products, thereby reversing the process and highlighting the materiality of the immaterial. [4]

In a similar way Aram Bartholl and Brody Condon have used virtual objects from speed racing games. In *Speed* (2006) Bartholl made a 1:1 scale sign with red flashing arrows and placed the sign in Bohnenstrasse, Bremen. The model of the arrows was found in the game Need for Speed Underground NFSU, where the red blinking signs lead the player on the right track. Brody Condon, on the other hand, made an exact replica of a Lamborghini Countach (1985), a model that he found in the game Need for Speed. The big difference was that the car was made of plastic branches, and the sculpture provided only the outline of a car – the "wireframe" in the language of 3D designers. What Bartholl and Condon do is investigating and problematizing the borderline between the virtual and the real by moving objects between these two worlds – worlds that are, today, more and more integrated and harder to distinguish.

Dutch artist Marieke Verbiesen is also mixing elements from both these worlds in her work *Pole Positon*. Pole Position was a racing game released in 1982 by Namco, and was one of the first games to use the rear-view racer format, where the player's view is behind and above the vehicle.

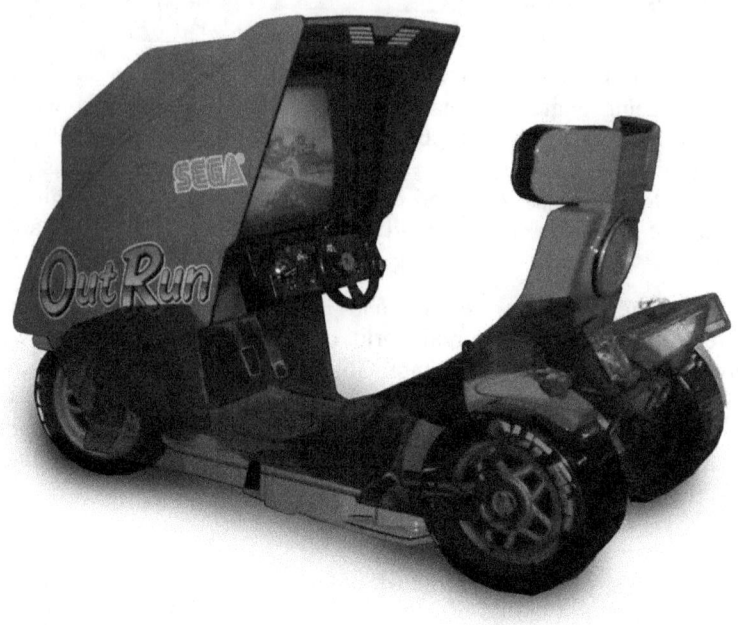

Garnet Hertz, *OutRun*, 2009 – 2012. Sketch of the cabinet with electric drivetrain. Image courtesy the artist.

In Verbiesen's installation, the setting of the game is generated by a realtime recording of a miniature landscape in perspective:

> Users look at a screen that combines both physical, realtime recorded elements, in a digital game with digital objects. They play the game with with a custom made joystick that controls a small real life car and moving elements in the installation competing against digitally generated objects in a race against time. The car and other mechanic objects are realtime recorded with a small camera which transports its signal to a computer that runs the game. Users see a screen where both digital and physical elements are visible and controllable in the game. [5]

The ultimate combination of real and virtual gameplay is found in Garnet Hertz's work *OutRun*. Some arcade versions of Outrun (Sega 1986) were presented in a red sit down cabinet that looked like a car. Garnet Hertz used this cabinet version as a model for his work, producing a video game system that actually drives. The system records the road in front of you and converts it into an 8-bit scenario:

> Where game simulations strive to be increasingly realistic (usually focused on graphics), this system pursue "real" driving through the game. Additionally, playing off the game-like experience one can have driving with an automobile navigation system, *OutRun* explores the consequences of using only a computer model of the world as a navigation tool for driving. [6]

One thing that you could not blame racing games for is air pollution. This is exactly what you can blame Eva and Franco Mattes for in the installation *Colorless, odorless and tasteless* (2011). They modified an old Pole Position game and installed a real engine in the arcade cabinet. When the player is driving the virtual car on the screen, the room is filled with carbon monoxide from the real engine. So, you not only run out of coins, but you are also gassed.

Lara Croft

"Does Lara Croft Wear Fake Polygons?" This was the question asked in 2000 by Anne-Marie Schleiner in a gender analysis essay of the popular video game Tomb Raider (Core Design, 1996). [7]

The reason for such an analysis was that the leading character of Tomb Raider, the British archaeologist Lara Croft, not only had big guns, but also big breasts. In a couple of years she became a well known character not only in the games world, but also for the general public when she entered the silver screen, played by Angelina Jolie. You could say that Lara Croft is the Mona Lisa of the game world: beautiful, mysterious and well known also by a wider audience.

In her essay, Schleiner also mentions the infamous *Nude Raider* patch, a game add-on that strips Lara Croft's clothing so you could play her naked.

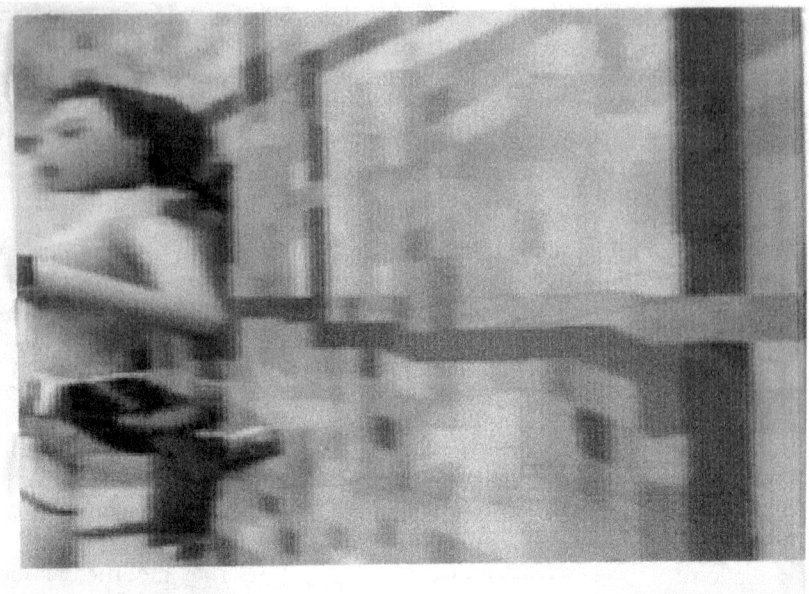

Miltos Manetas, *Untitled (Lara Croft)*, 1998. Vibracolour print on super glossy paper, courtesy the artist and Gloria Maria Gallery

The patch was further appropriated by artist Robert Nideffer in 1999, for his contribution to the exhibition "Cracking the Maze" curated by Schleiner. The project consisted of: an appropriated website where he repurposed the existing commercial site; a spoofed mail-server that re-routed messages sent by fans to the Director of development at Eidos UK as if they were coming from the Director of Marketing in the US branch; and a patched version of the Nude Raider patch, which placed police blotter style bar codes across Lara's private parts (and gave her a goatee as a Duchampian homage), thwarting the game player's expectation of seeing her polygonal private parts.

> This shows the male dominancy within the game world by having a female lead appearing like a super model. By presenting her naked, it makes the game seem satirical just pushing the creators' ideas a little further. [8]

Eidos responded by sending a cease and desist letter to the owners of nuderaider.com, the site that was hosting the Nude Raider patch, enforcing their copyright of Tomb Raider.

In the machinima *She Puppet* (2001), American artist Peggy Aswesh also investigates the gender and cultural identity of Lara Croft by mixing scenes from the Tomb Raider game. Aswesh describes Croft as a virtual girl-doll of the late 20th century, but "boy-doll" would be a better description since most of the player of the early Tomb Raider games were men or boys. In her essay Schleiner makes the observation that Lara Croft is a "well-trained techno-puppet created by and for the male gaze."

It's obvious that the video game Tomb Raider has played a major role in stirring up emotions with its obsolete and suspect attitude towards women. But Lara Croft has not only been a subject for critically engaged, artistic gender discussions. Artist Marieke Verbiesen has created the game *Tombraider 0.1* in which she flattened the 3D game into a 2D-world and borrowed aesthetic from the early game consoles. In the new game you could also find references to classic computer gaming experiences such as the stuck "loading" screen, bad language translations and space invader attacks.

It's not unusual that artist create copies of recent video games, with 3D hyperrealism graphic, in a retro old-fashioned style. Another way to do this is to use pixel-graphic. That is exactly what Arno Coenen, Rob Coenen and Rene Bosma did when they re-created the 3D game character into a 2D experience with a touch of pixel-feeling. The project *Output: 62.500 materialized pixels* used 62.500 pieces to create a floor mosaic measuring 5,25 x 5,25 meters of the video game icon Lara Croft. The mosaic has been exhibited at different places in Amsterdam and at Kiasma Museum in Helsinki, during the exhibition *Alien Intelligence* (2000).

So – fake polygons or not, it looks like Lara Croft has not only made an impression in the history of video games, but also in the history of art.

Grand Theft Auto (GTA)

The freedom to explore all of a game's territory is one of the keys to the success of the Grand Theft Auto (GTA) series from Rockstar Games. The first game in the series was released 1997. Since then, ten stand-alone games and four expansion packs has been produced for PC consoles, Xbox and Playstation devices.

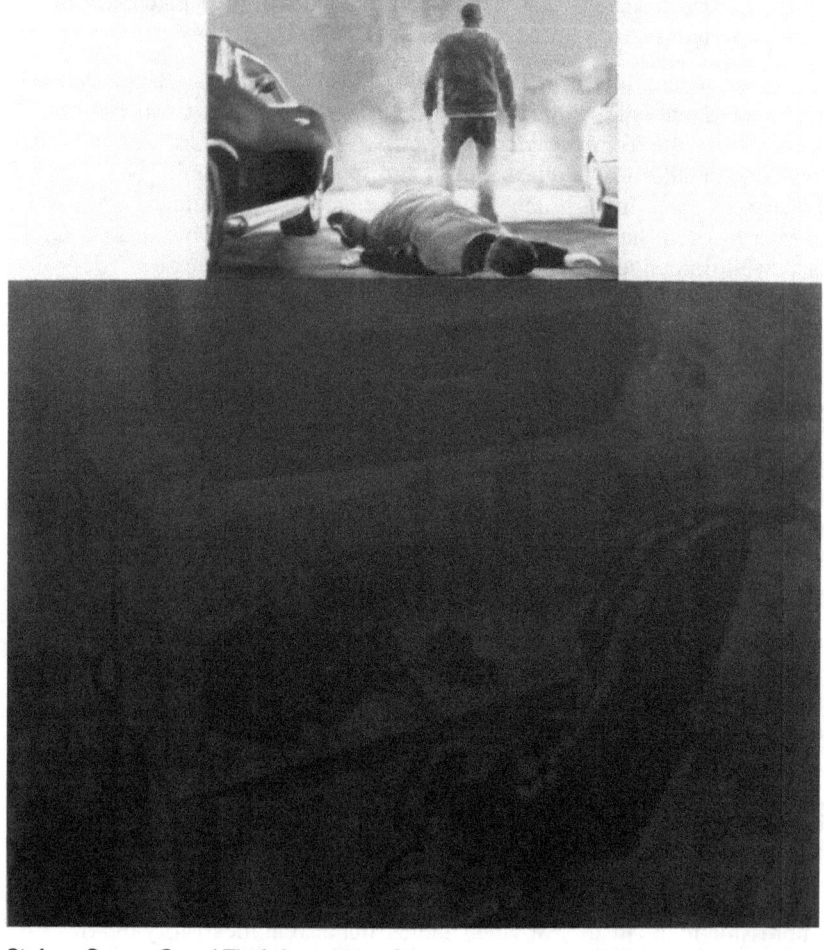

Stefano Spera, *Grand Theft Auto*, 2009. Oil on canvas, 120 x 100 cm. Courtesy Artra Gallery, Milan.

It's not only the players that love the freedom of the game's storyline – many artists have been attracted to GTA's virtual world and are inspired to explore it further, in their own ways. GTA is a good example how artists today are using different techniques to appropriate commercial video games for works of art.

But first, a distinction between fan art and game art may be useful. As in many popular cultures, there is a lot of fan art connected to video games that is created by dedicated players. That art can take the form of paintings, stories, videos and so on. But fan art is often only a reproduction of an existing game world. The fan artists are mimicking the aesthetic of the games and are following certain templates created by the fan community. Game art, on the other hand, experiments with and challenges the image and the idea of what a game can be. It can borrow the aesthetics of the game, but it is often critical of that aesthetic. The artists use the game as a platform or interface to explain and explore larger questions of gender, violence, and the economic and social realities that are played out in the game world.

One artist that has taken a critical view on the Grand Theft Auto series is the American Joan Pamboukes. In *The Enclosed Landscapes* series Pamboukes works with C-prints to create impressionist-style landscapes. The pictures are unfocused, with a limited color scale, and in some ways evoke Claude Monet's *Rouen Cathedral* series, which explored how the light changed on a church façade during the day. In Pamboukes's case, he raises the question of why the landscapes in video games such as GTA are so beautiful, in contrast to the ugly violence of the story.

I find it ironic that these beautifully serene landscapes were designed to house horrid simulations of unspeakable and appalling violence – a world where thievery, murder, warfare, and prostitution are the order of the day. Mesmerized by these atmospheric digital surroundings, I intended to capture and re-emphasize this intangible, sublime, and fleeting reality. [9]

The south African artist and researcher Pippa Tshabalala has also worked with photography in her series *Telling Death* (2009). Here, Tshabalala documented the deaths of different characters in Grand Theft Auto, and asked players to invent stories to explain how they died. Like many other works of game art, *Telling Death* explores the virtual violence and deaths gamers experience in virtual worlds. The project involves the gaming community, and asks participants to contribute fictional stories about the characters in a way that is also reminiscent of fan art.

It's also becoming common for artists to use video games as a motif for paintings. An example is provided by Italian artist Stefano Spera. His 2009 oil painting *Grand Theft Auto* is part of a series of paintings that documents the fictional world of pixels. On the painting's first panel we see a screen with a violent screenshot from GTA, and on the other panel, a child playing the game itself. In this painting Spera is playing with the contrast between the real and the virtual worlds, the innocent child and the violent society of adults.

Many virtual game worlds let you experience characters, environments, and situations that you would never be able to experience in normal life. For that purpose, the Finnish painter Petri Hytönen spent a year immersed in the virtual world of Grand Theft Auto looking for new inspiration for his art. The results was *GTA-SAGA*, a series of thirty large-scale watercolors with motifs and situations collected from GTA.

If you think painting sounds a bit anachronistic, you may enjoy newer expressions like machinima. In the past few years machinima have become more and more common among artists exploring the world of video games. Myfanwy Ashmore, an American artist, has created the video *Grand Theft Love Song* where the main GTA character Nico Bellic is dancing in his safe house. In some ways, the video disarms the violent character by turning him into a puppet forced to dance to the 1927 song "Creole Love Call". David Borawski has also created a machinima based on the world of GTA. This is how he describes the video *Burn Out / Erased by the First Rain* (2009):

> *Burn Out / Erased by the First Rain* is comprised of two sequences staged and recorded from within the game GTA – San Andreas. The virtual biker does an extended circular burn out, using the motorcycle's image of freedom and rebellion as a starting point, yet alluding to the repetition and futility of contemporary society." [10]

First published as a series of articles on *Furtherfield.org* in 2010 – 2011.

[1] From *Wikipedia*, http://en.wikipedia.org/wiki/Appropriation.

[2] From the exhibition flyer. "pong.mythos", curated by Andreas Lange, February 11 - April 30, 2006. More info: http://pong-mythos.net/.

[3] Mathias Jannson, "Playing "Tetris with Michael Johansson", in *Gamescenes.org*, August 17, 2010.

[4] Artists' statement, originally available at www.objectsofvirtualdesire.com.

[5] Artist's statement, available at http://poleposition.marieke.nu/.

[6] Cf. http://www.conceptlab.com/outrun/.

[7] Anne-Marie Schleiner, "Does Lara Croft wear fake polygons? Gender Analysis of the 3rd Person shooter/adventure game with female heroine and Gender Role Subversion in the Game Patch", in *Switch*, 2000, online at www.opensorcery.net/lara2.html.

[8] Artist's statement, online at http://dimension.ucsd.edu/~mazearcheology/nideffer.html.

[9] Artist's statement, available at http://joanpamboukes.com/.

[10] Artist's statement, available at https://vimeo.com/15823124.

INTERVIEWS

Pippin Barr

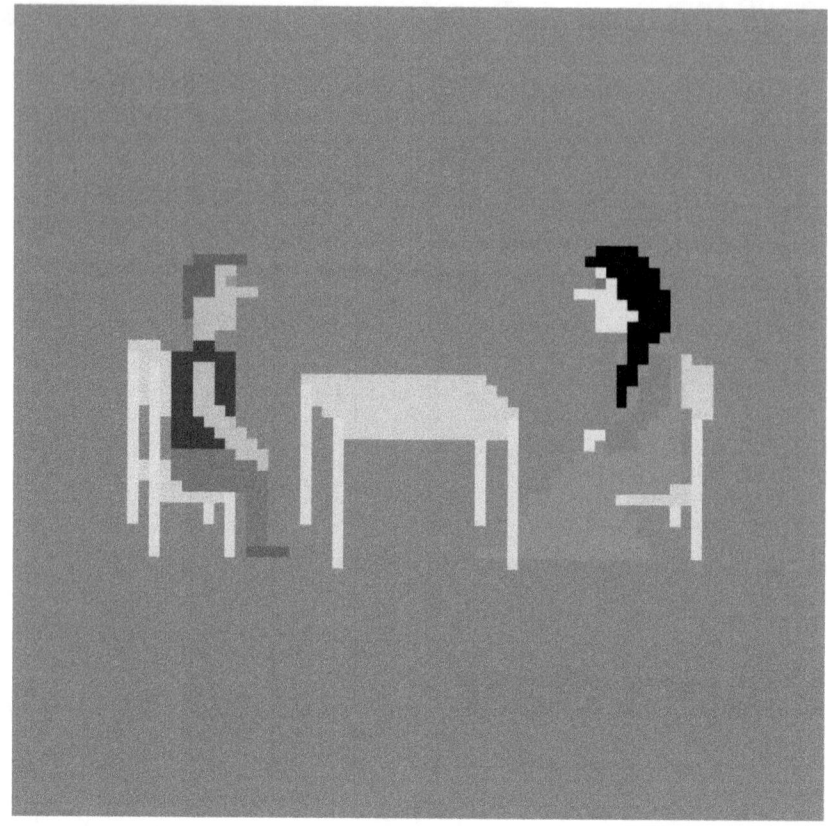

Pippin Barr, *The Artist Is Present,* 2011. Image courtesy the artist.

Pippin Barr (http://www.pippinbarr.com/) is currently working and teaching at the Center for Computer Game Research at IT University of Copenhagen in Denmark. He has a Ph.D. and wrote his dissertation about "video game values", that is about how human values are promoted, either overtly or subtly, in the games we play. He frequently blogs about video games and has recently started to create his own games - games that in short time have caught the indie games scenes attention. This interview focuses on the controversial game *The Artist Is Present* (2011), inspired by the performance by Marina Abramović with the same name, presented at MoMA, New York in 2010.

Mathias Jansson: In your game *The Artist Is Present* you recreated a performance by artist Marina Abramovi , presented at the Museum of Modern Art in New York 2010. What's your own relationship to Abramovi 's art and why did choose to turn this particular performance into a game?

Pippin Barr: On one level the decision to make a game of *The Artist Is Present* was just on a whim – it seemed intuitively clear that it would be fun and funny to produce a game version of such an important piece of contemporary art. I didn't see the performance when it happened, but certainly followed it while it was going on and was fascinated not just by the work itself (two people sitting opposite each other, looking into each other's eyes) but the surrounding aspects too: the giant queues, the celebrities, the controversies, the artists who performed in the performance, and so on. It's definitely a work that was a lot larger than "just" itself.

Looking back, it's fairly obvious that performance art is a good choice when you're trying to represent an artwork in a game, and that Abramović's piece is particularly good because it had certainly game-like qualities: crucially, it's *participatory*... The audience is a genuine part of it (one at a time!). You really need to have that quality if you want to make a more "literal" game version – a literal version of Duchamp's Fountain, say, would be really boring, just an image of the piece and perhaps the ability to walk around it. (Which is not to say my own game isn't boring – it certainly can be.)

So it was the "procedural" elements of the work that appealed from a game making perspective. And as I said, not just the performance itself, which is fairly low interaction from a game perspective (you look into her eyes), but also the surrounding elements of queuing and getting there early and so on. And in fact they became the main "mechanic" of the game, because it was the committed *waiting* and relationship to time that interested me the most from a design perspective. Waiting is such a no-no in games (Narthex is a notable exception and there are others, like Desert Bus), it's regarded as so abusive, and yet it's a major part of life. To the extent we want games to (sometimes) be "about life", waiting is fair game.

In your games *Safety Instructions* (2011) and *The Artist Is Present* you describe the graphics as "Sierra-style", after Sierra Entertainment, a video-game developer very active in the eighties. Why do you (and many other indie game developers) choose to work with the style of old video games instead of adopting the photo-realistic approach used in the commercial game scene?

Pippin Barr: Interesting question. Funnily enough, when I started "seriously" making games early this year I swore to myself I'd stay away from these pixel-style graphics because I was tired of seeing them as the house-style of indie games. My game *GuruQuest* went at least some way toward a different graphical style.

I used the kind of "Sierra" style for the last two games for different reasons. With *Safety Instructions* I knew I was going to be doing a lot of animation, which is not something I have much experience with. My original concept was to much more closely mirror the instructional design style of the actual instructions cards – very smooth lines with just enough information to communicate. But animating that kind of aesthetic, and in fact just producing it in the first place, isn't really in my skill set. In going to a "low res" view I gained the chance to represent the same kinds of images much more straightforwardly. In a literal sense, there are fewer pixels involved! This becomes doubly true when you're animating – the difference between animating a 300×300 pixel image, say, and the 50×50 pixel images I was working with is enormous and beyond me. By using fewer pixels I had fewer decisions to make in each frame, fewer details to represent, and so on. It made life easier and, as a side effect, ended up looking nice (I think).

With *The Artist Is Present* I much more consciously chose the Sierra/AGI look as a part of the game's inner and outer aesthetics. It's not just that I wanted it to look like a Sierra game (kind of a "what if Sonny Bonds from *Police Quest* went to MoMA?") but also in some ways catch on to some of the interactions. Sierra games from that era were very unforgiving and unapologetic – *Police Quest* in particular is one of my favourite games and it has this obsession with procedure – doing things right. Make sure you read suspects their rights, handcuff them in the right way, and on and on. That felt related to what I was doing with *The Artist Is Present* – it's a game about following the rules (in this case the rules of a performance and the gallery space it's in).

On the other hand, it backfired to the degree that some players familiar with the Sierra style felt it implied there would be puzzles to solve, so when the museum was closed, for instance, they immediately felt there must be some way to break in, when there isn't. So the visual aesthetics of these games speaks hugely to player expectations and to the kinds of underlying mechanics they might have (though of course it doesn't *have* to be this way).

How do you experience the development and interest for independent video games during the last years? And how do you like to contribute to the indie game scene?

Pippin Barr: Huh... well I'm very new to this world, and I really don't even characterise myself as an independent developer, at least not to myself. I started making games at the start of this year because I've researched them for a number of years and began to feel that for me personally there was something a little off about thinking about games all the time but never making them. Perhaps because I have degrees in computer science and know how to program (if not all that well), it seemed absurd for me to spend all this time talking about games, playing them, critiquing them, wishing they were different, without making them myself.

As such I'm not really "part" of anything I think of as a community of designers and developers, though I like the idea of that. I think the indie games scene is just amazing and I'm deeply impressed by the projects I see out there. In some ways it doesn't really need any "contributions" in the sense of helping it along – it's just happening, people are making games... in some ways it's an unstoppable force.

Of course, this comes from my personal perspective which is that, for now, I'm completely happy just making the little games I want to make and putting them out there. I'm not making any money or asking for it. I can imagine that if I was wanting to rely on making games for an income things would be radically different and I'd have a different view – but for now I'm able to teach and so on at university and my wife has a more stable career, also as a games academic.

Your academic expertise is "video game values". What does it mean? And do you see any difference in values between indie games and commercial games?

Pippin Barr: Funny to think about that – my Ph.D. dissertation seems like it was a long time ago now. And yet I do still think about games at least partly in those terms. In my dissertation my interest was in the idea that games communicate values (that is, an idea of "preferable conduct") through their various aspects (aesthetics, mechanics, social setting, etc.) and that this was an important way to look at what games are and do – in my case from the perspective of human-computer interaction. Ian Bogost has written very eloquently and well about these kinds of ideas, of course, particularly in his *Persuasive Games* [1] book.

I still think about those aspects of games, but my attention has turned much more toward thinking about the kinds of experiences people have with games and could have with games. One of the courses I teach at my university is "experimental interaction", where I try to help (and convince!) the students to go away from conventional design practices to find something new. Generally by bombarding them with as many different ideas as possible.

As to value difference between indie and commercial games – it's inevitable that they're there. At the most obvious level, indie games take risks and, by and large, commercial games just don't. There's not a lot of money in risky, unusual, and "alternative values" games. That's part of why, by and large, indie games are so much more expressive (and for me interesting) than commercial games. The range of values an indie might want to promote or embed in his or her game is just so much larger than commercial producers could dream of – when something like "No Russian" [2] or calling one team the Taliban [3] is the height of controversy, you really have a long way to go in terms of commercial games taking risks. Meanwhile, games like *Super Columbine Massacre RPG!* Or *Beautiful Escape* are really going for it in terms of risk and values. Whether or not we like them or want to play them, it can't be denied these games are doing things large-scale commercial games may never manage.

And that's probably alright, too – not everything has to be mainstream. Still, wouldn't hurt if some of the indie spirit rubbed off a bit more (okay, a lot more) on the commercial world – and that includes the player bases of commercial games, who are just as much a part of the system that keeps producing the same small set of ideas each year. Myself included!

First published on *Next-Level* in November 2011 with the title "Pippin Barr – The artist is present".

[1] Ian Bogost, *Persuasive Games. The Expressive Power of video games*, MIT Press, 2007.
[2] "No Russian" is the fourth mission of Call of Duty: Modern Warfare 2 (Activision 2009). The mission sees the player take part in an airport massacre of hundreds of civilians, and made Call of Duty: Modern Warfare 2 one of the most controversial games to date.
[3] In August 2010, it was announced that the upcoming Medal of Honor, to be released in October 2010 by Electronic Arts, would have allowed the player to play as Talibans. After a huge outcry, the feature was removed.

Nils Deneken

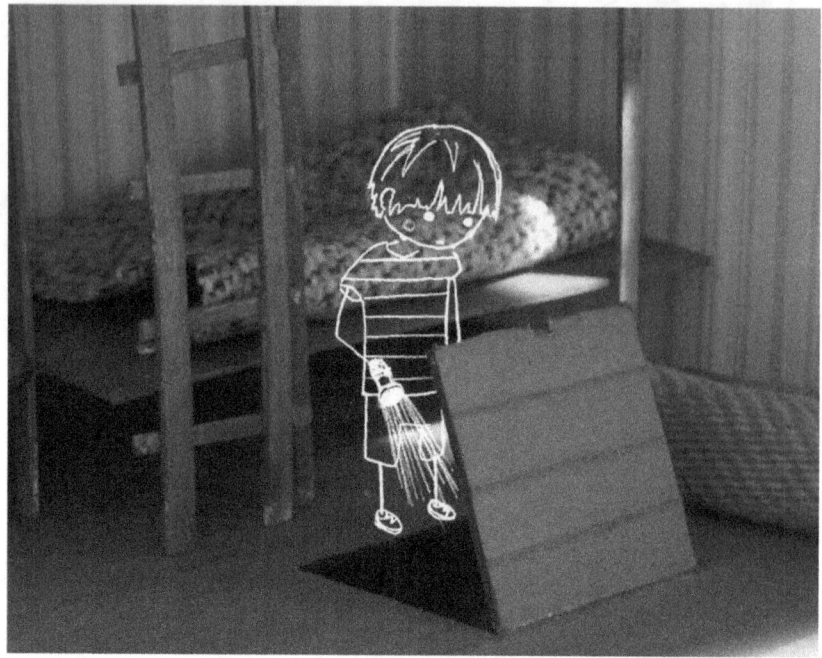

Die Gute Fabrik, *Rückblende*, 2006. Screenshot, courtesy the artists.

Die Gute Fabrik (http://gutefabrik.com/) is a small games studio based in Copenhagen, Denmark. According to their website, they take classic play forms from the past – be they physical folk games from the playground or adventure games from old consoles – and breathe new life into them with 21st century technology and their own sense of style and storytelling. We strive to develop games that are hand-crafted, synaesthetic, offbeat, and above all, personal.

Mathias Jansson: What is the history behind Die Gute Fabrik?

Nils Deneken: I founded Die Gute Fabrik in 2008 while I was hiking around the Fjords of Copenhagen. It was just an abandoned factory back then, but I liked the view and moved in. It's a really nice base to work on projects, since it's quiet and the nature around this place is quite spectacular. Bernie Schulenburg stayed here for a while and we worked on *Where is my Heart?* together. Recently I was joined by Douglas Wilson, the Designer of *Johann Sebastian Joust*, who became my partner in running the firm. We're both cofounders of the Copenhagen Game Collective and have been working together on several projects, among others *B.U.T.T.O.N.* And *5 minute mmorpg*. Since we value each other's work a lot, it made sense to join up and run this studio together.

Why are you so interested in recycling old game concepts?

Nils Deneken: The games we're interested in are rooted in the past, be it folk games or video game concepts from our youth, but we both have the feeling that you could take those concepts and create something unique with the knowledge and technology we have today. I'm not talking about just recycling old game concepts, but move them into entirely new directions. It seems that in the evolution of games a lot of possibilities have been neglected, and we'd like to have a second look at those missed opportunities.

The game *Johann Sebastian Joust* was part of the art exhibition "Space Invaders" at the Nikolaj Contemporary Art Center in the beginning of 2012. Can you tell me about the game and why do you think it was selected to be exhibited in an art hall?

Nils Deneken: *Johann Sebastian Joust* is a no-graphics, digitally-enabled folk game for 2 to 7 players, designed for motion controllers (such as the PlayStation Move). Each player has a controller in their hands, once they move the controllers too fast, they're out. The sensitivity of the controller is tied to the speed of music, so when the music is running in slow motion, the player has to move extra slow to survive. When the music speeds up, this threshold becomes less strict, giving the players a small window to dash at their opponents. Channel the power of J.S. Bach, and try to jostle your opponents' controllers while protecting your own. The last person standing is the winner.

The game was selected for the exhibition, since it goes beyond the traditional players demography. People who have no experience in video games can pick up *J.S. Joust* and have fun with it. Instead of the players and spectators looking at the screen, they look at each other and automatically get into contact. It's basically a very immediate social experience where there's no filter, like a screen or some interface between the participants, which is quite rare for digital games these days.

What qualities do you think a video game should have to be an interesting work of art?

Nils Deneken: If it breaks with the conventions of the medium in some way and expands the understanding of the observer of what games can be or if it's just really, really beautiful.

Both *Where is my heart?* and *Rückblende* are based on a childhood memory. The childhood is a common theme in literature and film, but how can personal experiences and memories from a person's childhood be used in video games?

Nils Deneken: Video games are among other things a good storytelling medium, but it works quite differently from a book or a movie. As long as you can involve the player and make the player feel as a part of the story, you can pretty much make a game about any topic. I think it's important that the players don't feel too much that the story is forced on them, but that they can discover it by themselves.

What's your experience of the indie game scene in Copenhagen?

Nils Deneken: The game jams at the Copenhagen IT University each year are great, and with the Copenhagen Game Collective we tried to arrange some events and bring our games to the public, which worked ok so far, but we still have a long way to go. Besides the collective, I'm seldom participating in social game industry events in Copenhagen. There are some really talented indie developers in Copenhagen, but I don't know them well personally, so I'm actually not sure whether we have a scene here. I hope that this will develop over time, though.

And how do you see the future for indie game developers?

Nils Deneken: Hard to predict the future. It's easy enough to release a game these days, but it's hard to make a living of it, especially if you want to stay independent.

First published in *Next-Level* in January 2012 with the title "Nils Deneken from Die Gute Fabrik".

Constant Dullart

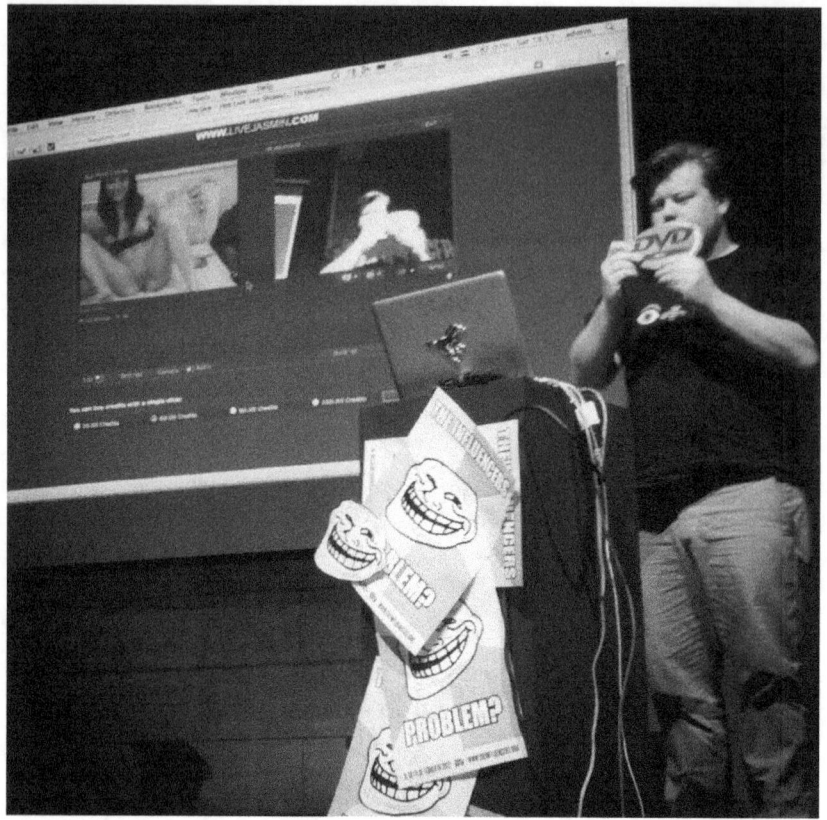

Constant Dullaart performing *DVD Screensaver* at The Influencers Festival, Barcelona 2012.

When I heard about the Easter egg that makes the Google search page rotate when you type "do a barrell" in the search field, I thought: "Hey, wait a minute, this is old news. Constant Dullaart already did it with *therevolvinginternet.com*!"

Constant Dullaart is an artist that – in the tradition of net artists like JODI - investigates and questions well known interfaces on the internet. He flips, bends and rotates sites as Google and Youtube to challenge our view of the internet services we use every day. Like a poet, Dullaart investigates the internet grammar and software dialects, and make us aware of the new sides of this visual language that we often take for granted. On Youtube you can find a series of videos where Dullaart searches for impossible search strings like "][-[" or "rw4tbtb" or "-=-". The search always returns the same sentence: "Your search - - did not match any documents." The videos could be interpreted as a metaphor for the "law of instruments", a law that is more familiarly under the phrase "if all you have is a hammer, everything looks like a nail". If you always use Google to search for information on the internet, your world will be googlefied and everything on the net will look like nails, but if you use the whole toolbox of different search tools you will find both screws and nuts on the net.

In this interview Constant Dullaart talks about his art and his recent participation in Transmediale 2012, where he also presented a new project with the ambition to preserve online digital art for the future.

Mathias Jansson: On the 18th of January you and many other artists followed Wikipedia's example and blacked out your homepage as a protest against the SOPA act [1]. You also made the page *thecensoredinternet.com,* that displays censored search results from Google. As an artist using and remixing material from different sources on the internet, what's your position in the ongoing discussion about copyright on the internet?

Constant Dullaart: I do view copyright as doing much more wrong than good, and in a crude comparison, I view it like the most organized religious systems. Therefore the Kopimism [2] initiative seems to be a completely relevant response in this case, since copyright has become as powerful as a religion in western culture. Holy Disney for example, did not only found an art school (Calarts), the company was also at the foundations of a fortified copyright legislation in the United States that prevents the same art school students from actively responding and engaging with the culture around them that has become so much more dynamic through the addition of the web. By falsely constructing the idea of a prolonged intellectual property, this legislation created a demon. The idea that an industry can make money through limiting access to content not made by them, is not that even that old, but it is very reluctant in the days when it has become technologically obsolete, by now it is even halting technical progress.

Most people I know are watching movies and documentaries, that they normally wouldn't have been able to see since the legal distribution channels are simply not capable of delivering such tailored content, especially when they live abroad. The lack of innovation on the side of the copyright industry is shocking, how slow initiatives like Spotify [3] and other distribution systems are allowed to work in Germany for example is staggering. Half of the YouTube links I receive from friends are blocked when I view them from a German IP address. Next to that law firms here keep ripping people off by sending them threat letters and fake fines. I do think culture as a whole is changing, and we need to be able to use previous people's additions to culture as building blocks for our own. It's enormously embarrassing that a corporate international lobby from the copyright industry and money that was made over the backs of people like Robert Johnson, or Bo Diddley (to name just a few ripped off personal heroes) is trying to prevent us from standing on the shoulders of giants. In these days of technological advancement we do not have need to have our culture held for ransom by price agreements, and lazy distribution moguls.

This is why I basically try to avoid content owned by these larger copyright holders, and I believe everyone should do the same. Avoid any content of people that complain about piracy like the plague would be my advice. Perhaps it's not hard to draw the comparison to renaissance times here. Artists had to find new distribution channels and audiences to liberate themselves from the power of the Catholic church. Do with my work as you please, just do not ad any form of copyright to it. And if you're nice, you will mention the source of your inspiration in or with the new work. Like you would do in a blog post with a trackback. I think the web is a perfect place to respond to each others works, and let them co-exist, as responses. Copying is not stealing, the original is intact, and money shall be made in different ways.

> In your art you are trying to visualise the internet grammar and software dialects, in a way that reminds me of JODI's work. Is JODI an inspiration for you, or where else do you find inspiration?

Constant Dullaart: Yes, JODI are living legends, every time they give me a compliment I can't help but think it's sarcastic, I feel like Jimmy Hendrix just told a kid he strummed a nice chord. But they're more punk of course, and most of the time they give me a compliment by bitching about how good a work was I made, I guess they mean well. But my inspiration I find within simple formal play mostly, this could be from Gordon Matta-Clark to Finn Hendil [4], but also on the street, and mostly in the possibility or impossibility of a visual idea, a software option, a new service, tool, or code. Of course I could name drop all you want here, but to tell you the truth, I go hard on demo videos.

> In your works *baselitz.org*, *internetspread.com*, *thedis-agreeinginternet.com* and *therevolvinginternet.com* you work

with simple methods as flipping the page and rotating it in order to change the viewer's perspective on everyday internet services. What's the idea behind these works?

Constant Dullaart: To influence a persons view on things, to alter a perception of a concept or representation seems to be a very basic description of what a contemporary artist does. This can be done in all sorts of ways and through all sorts of emotions, but hopefully making you aware of the different viewpoints and the dynamics of that certain concept or representation. Since most of the representation of the world around us is consumed through the world wide web, the web seems the right place to do this as a contemporary artist, right?

Seeing that over 80 percent of the people that use web pages (outside of Facebook) access it through Google, I decided to manipulate the most common startpage, including all potential pages afterwards. I was re editing all kinds of movies and video material, but now I found a way to re edit any content requested by the viewer. My mind blew at this potential. All of the works you named are sites that existed already, that already had a reason to be there, they had an alibi. I stopped believing that I needed to add brand new content to the world a long time ago, I think we are needed in framing this enormous amount of visual language that is developing and we are overloaded with before we have figured out what it all entails... Click scroll swipe click mispelllling lol wtf clikc tty.

In *Youtube on the Floor*, you sit on the floor and move circles to create the effect of the loading icon of Youtube. Furthermore, in the DVD screensaver performance you use a DVD sign to create a performance about the floating DVD sign you can see on the screen when your DVD is inactive. Why did you choose to go off-line?

Constant Dullaart: Of course there is a friction, which is essentially very formal and perhaps literal. It is also easily confused to be a tribute to the impact of the original environment of the icon. Take the giant *Map* marker by Aram Bartholl, this is a very direct translation, which works on this previously described friction, its funny to suddenly see this visual rhetoric misplaced, and hopefully makes you think of the signifiers and rethorics you are used to in daily life. In these works of mine I enjoyed emphasizing the human aspect of these enormous corporate entities we are interacting with day by day by adding a high dose of bricolage to the videos.

The DVD logo IS designed by someone (if you want to figure this out you need to pay thousands of dollars and sign a non disclosure agreement by the looks of it). The hole in a DVD is as large as the old Dutch 10 cent coin, since the original CD was designed by Phillips. These small decisions that impact so many people fascinate me. And just think about all the people slaving away making funny video's that should become memes one day, addicted to the potential likes of their audience. Thinking of their best Facebook status update yet, and in what tone they should comment to make it successful.

And think of the people that designed the logo's and made the decisions at YouTube (Google) for example. Who decided to put this play-button in the player. Was there a vote in the board of directors or something? (if there was, design FAIL) These website's are not these anonymous magical entities that they are made out to be. They are run by people that can make mistakes. Google is not a computer .

You took part in Transmediale 2012 in Berlin. What were you showing there and how important are festivals like Transmediale for you as a net artist?

Constant Dullaart: The work I have showed in this year Transmediale was a video out of my HEALED series, where I used Adobe Photoshop's spot healing brush to 'Heal" disasters. This work is made to show the dichotomy of a software manufacturer choosing names to describe tools that influence the representation of reality, and reality itself. In this case I 'healed' every frame of the first video recording of the fire on the BP oil platform "deep water horizon" (April 20, 2010) The sound was left as it was originally, so the work consists of abstract, out of focus color fields moving around the screen with the soundtrack of a loud helicopter engine. The video was uploaded to YouTube as a response to the original recording.

But next to this I also officially launched the "documenting and archiving of internet activities" initiative *net.artdatabase.org* with Robert Sakrowsky (with a conscious wink to the net.art movement in the URL, yes). Basically to encourage the use of simple and subjective documentation of online art works, that are lost while the discussion goes on how these works can be best archived. Documenting them as if they were performances in a public space, with viewing context included. I love how these documentations turn out, the awkward interactions of the viewer with the work and the necessary hardware, typing with two fingers, waiting while the noisy computer finishes loading the page. Soon enough the only way we will see this kind of interactions with artworks will be through documentation. And seeing that the social context in and around the network will never be possible to download or archived, I believe it proper archiving should not even be attempted.

First published on Digimag, Issue 62, March 2012, with the title "Law Of The Instrument. An Interview with Constant Dullart".

[1] "The Stop Online Piracy Act (SOPA) is a United States bill introduced by U.S. Representative Lamar S. Smith (R-TX) to expand the ability of U.S. law enforcement to fight online trafficking in copyrighted intellectual property and counterfeit goods. Provisions include the requesting of court orders to bar advertising networks and payment facilities from conducting business with infringing websites, and search engines from linking to the websites, and court orders requiring Internet service providers to block access to the websites." From *Wikipedia*, http://en.wikipedia.org/wiki/Stop_Online_Piracy_Act.

[2] "The Missionary Church of Kopimism, founded by 19-year-old philosophy student Isak Gerson, is a congregation of file sharers who believe that copying information is a sacred virtue. The Church, based in Sweden, has been officially recognized [...] as a religious community, after three application attempts." From *Wikipedia*, http://en.wikipedia.org/wiki/Missionary_Church_of_Kopimism.

[3] "Spotify is a Swedish music streaming service offering digitally restricted streaming of selected music from a range of major and independent record labels, including Sony, EMI, Warner Music Group, and Universal. Launched in October 2008 by Swedish startup Spotify AB, the service had approximately ten million users as of 15 September 2010, about 2.5 million of who were paying members". From *Wikipedia*, http://en.wikipedia.org/wiki/Spotify.

[4] Finn Hendil is one of the men behind the famous Philips PM5544 Test Pattern, one of the test cards most commonly used by TV companies.

Jakub Dvorsky

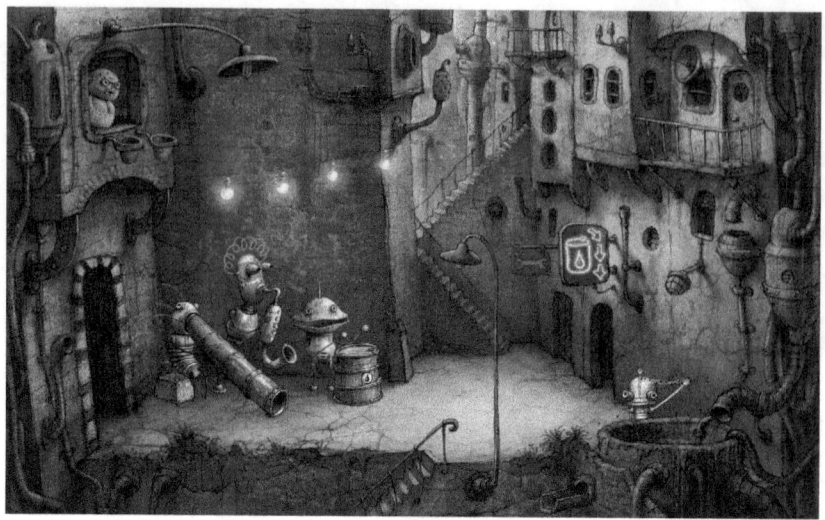

Amanita Design, *Machinarium*, 2009. Wallpaper

Jakub Dvorsky is the creator of the point-and-click adventure game *Samorost*, published in 2003. Today he is working as a Game Designer and Graphic Artist for Amanita Design (http://amanita-design.net/), a small independent video game development studio based in the Czech Republic.

Mathias Jansson: You made *Samorost* when you still were a student at the Academy of Arts in Prague. How was the attitude towards games and art games back then?

Jakub Dvorsky: I studied at the studio of animated film where we learned how to make classical animated films with puppets, cut-out animation or hand-drawn animation. At that time only a few people in our studio were using computers for animating and I was the first one who tried to create an interactive film or game. We used to have a lot of freedom in our school so it wasn't a big issue to create a game instead of film as my thesis project but it sparked some discussion. Generally older teachers thought the interactivity is breaking narrative while younger people thought the game is interesting and games as an artistic medium should be taken more seriously.

Where do you find inspirations for your games and art?

Jakub Dvorsky: A lot of inspiration comes directly from nature and also from human creations which are in some form of decay – old rusty machines, abandoned factories and industrial buildings overgrown with grass etc. Besides that we are of course influenced by many older games, films, books, music records, paintings etc. Basically you can find some inspiration almost everywhere, important is to have your eyes and mind open and that's not always easy.

What did Amanita Design 's success mean for the indie game scene in the Czech Republic?

Jakub Dvorsky: I'm not sure as I don't know much about Czech indie scene. However I know a few developers from Slovakia, Russia or Germany who are directly influenced by our games.

Amanita Design's latest game *Machinarium* will be available for iPad. How did the last year's explosion of smartphones and handheld devices affect you as game developer?

Jakub Dvorsky: We don't care very much about new technologies so we are staying calm :) Unfortunately, smartphones have small screens even though the resolution is high, therefore we are not interested in developing for it at the moment but we are definitely interested in tablets which are perfect for our kind of games. It's similar to reading a book – you can do it on the train, on the couch, in your bed and that's great of course. Besides tablets we are also interested in bringing our new games to, at least one, of the bigger consoles so people can enjoy it on their big TV or even better on hi-res projection.

First published in *Next-Level* in October 2011, with the title "Jakub Dvorsky creator of Samorost".

Sachiko Hayashi

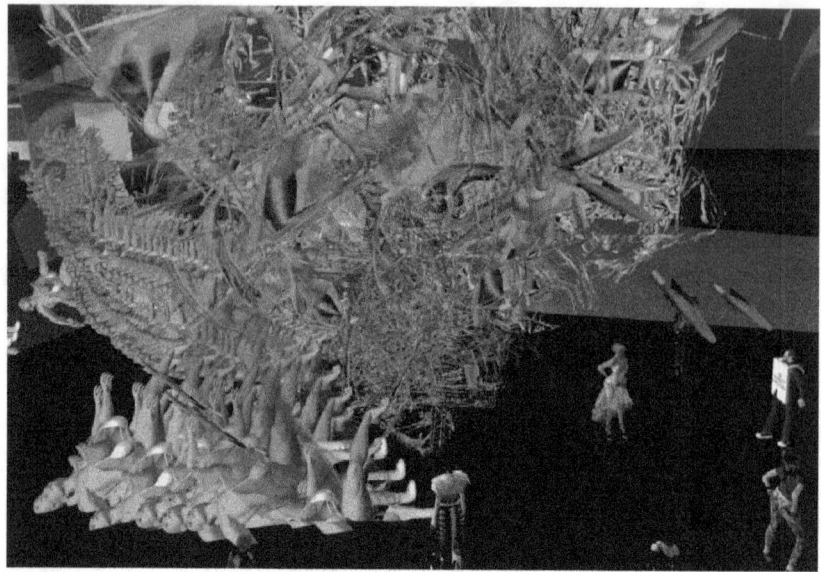

Alan Sondheim's Yoshikaze "Up-In-The-Air" residency project. Image courtesy Yoshikaze

Sachiko Hayashi is a visual artist who primarily works in video and screen-based interactive media. She is from Tokyo and has lived in the US and UK, but she is currently based in Sweden. Her video works, an investigation of temporal composition in subjective imagery, often in combination with audio-visual experimentation, have won wide recognition internationally over the years. In 1991 she founded MASH, an art duo, with EAM composer Magnus Alexanderson, to investigate various audio-visual combinations. She is also the founder of the internet network DIAN and since 2003 she is the chief editor of *Hz-journal*, a web journal by the non-profit art organization Fylkingen, based in Stockholm.

Hayashi's works exhibit a unique blend of aesthetic and conceptual foundation with the use of technology, as she consistently explores co-relation between image, sound, conceptualisation in art, and discourses in philosophy and other social disciplines. She is best known for her net art that involves examination of human nature with high use of interactivity, in which not only the retrieved intricate picture of its subject becomes its focus but also our own reaction toward what is being revealed through interactivity.

Together with HUMLab in Umeå, Sweden, she started in 2010 Yoshikaze "Up-In-The-Air", a residency program in Second Life. In this interview she elaborates her ideas about her own art and Second Life as a platform for artistic experiments.

Mathias Jansson: Since the middle of the nineties, you have been working with interactive media. What, in the beginning, made you so interested in these media?

Sachiko Hayashi: Spatial and temporal movement of impact and influence embodied in interactivity has always been fascinating to me. Just like a stone cast into a pond creates ripples in the water, one movement generates another, inducing change by triggering another phenomenon in both space and time.

The first artwork which I wanted to show in public clearly indicated this fascination. The work, called *Resonance*, was developed in 1989-90 and was an interactive sound installation. The work would consist of yellow plastic tubes of about 15 cm in diameter, with lights strategically placed to illuminate the tubes from their insides. About 15-20 of these plastic tubes would stand on the floor to create an artificial forest, inside which several sensors would be placed to register the movements of visitors. A small speaker would be assigned to each sensor, which, once activated, would trigger randomly-selected sounds and short sound compositions via a computer into its assigned speaker. It was an ambitious project, not only because I was a beginner but also because it would have involved a programmer, a sound artist/composer, and a lot of material and equipments, all of which were very costly back then. In the end, due to the lack of financial support, the project never became materialised.

This experience made me aware of the financial aspect of involvement of technology, an awareness which still persists in everything I do today. For example, I do programming for all my works. It isn't that I like to code but that it has to do with the bitter experience that I could not secure the funding for a programmer in the above described project. The more you can do yourself, the less dependent you are when it comes to financing of projects, and the risk involved due to financial difficulties becomes less. That was the lesson I learned.

Net Art has been a part of this direction I have taken. In the middle of the '90s I enrolled in a Master's programme in UK which, among other things, taught me how to programme for CD-ROM projects. Because of the small scale of CD-ROM project management and its inexpensive nature, I could reignite my interest in interactivity. From there, to enter into the online arena when the Internet became truly available as a media platform was a natural progression.

Which main issues interest you as an artist?

Sachiko Hayashi: My answer to your question is both simple and complex at the same time. Art practice has always been for me a search to get to know myself in my own terms. Each of my works represents various aspect of that search. What I aspire to find in the end is my own adequate way to express who I am in my wholeness, wherein my personal experience, including racial, cultural, generational as well as individual, can be manifested in a crystallised manner as work of art.

Let me elaborate: As a non-white and non-Westerner and woman who has also spent more than half of her life abroad in the West, my experience is naturally different from those whose race, gender, culture and tradition are accepted as mainstream. Wherever I am, even in my own native country, I am a perpetual stranger finding myself on the periphery.

The perpetual peripheries (or the Other, to use a term from Postmodern philosophy) risk seeing themselves through the eyes of the center, even when that clearly leads to denying one's own experience and at times eradicating one's own perspective. This condition for my own existence has led me to problematisation of the self as well as questioning of definitions, categories, and even languages of genres.

My constant attraction to areas of new art activities probably stems from this existence. I see freedom in the chaos of the unestablished. This attitude has resulted in various categories of expression, of which the use of video is one, sound another, net art yet another, as well as installation and audio-visual performance, since my focus has never been about what falls into what category but a question of my own existence. In short, I am not a genre-oriented artist. I am more interested in the thread that binds my work together at a deeper level.

Although one common denominator of all my works since the mid '90s has been the use of technology, I believe it is safe to say I differ from many of the people who are interested in New Media. My felt attraction has always lain in the fluidity of the not-yet-established, its room for deviations and deflections, and never in the presumed moral high ground of novelty. In that sense, it is unfortunate for me that New Media has today become an area where worship of science and reminiscent Modernistic monism prevail predominantly; as where they see a future, I tend to see the past, and where they see a liberation, I tend to see the oppression.

The development of new media and technology has been very fast in the last 20 years. How working with that tool kit has affected you as an artist?

Sachiko Hayashi: Technology, especially new technology, is always changing as you point out. Only until a decade ago even the platform (computer operating systems) was in constant development so a work created on one platform couldn't be run when its operating system became obsolete. An application (authoring tool) goes out of circulation by a management decision of a company, and by the same token new applications and programming languages surface that are more fitting to the need of the day. Furthermore a new arena can be created, and with it a set of new investigations can begin, as it was the case with the Internet and its networked space.

This in its turn creates an environment that is different from traditional media; in traditional media the depth of knowledge and skills are somewhat constant, whereas the areas that embody new technology are much more unstable, often with the effect that the quest for the new is being given the first priority in the face of changing technology. In short, technocentrism, where evaluation of works is based on the newest and most complicated technological inventiveness, is a common feature of New Media. And the feeling of keeping oneself a jour with the new can be annoyingly stressful, constantly leaving one the impression of never being able to devote sufficient time to deepen and solidify one's aesthetic ground, let alone one's skills.

This condition inevitably creates certain problematics specific to New Media; application of new technology can overshadow artistic expressions, and the tendency exists to invite works that are more on the verge of technological and design development. It is also true that a work based on the topic of the day (new trend in technology) would not survive the test of time as art. One such example is Laser Art, to which a chapter of Frank Popper's book on Electronic Art is dedicated. While laser has become a wide-spread common medium for large scale spectacles, the practitioners who saw its potential in artistic endeavour are today largely forgotten. Pursuit of new technology can make you a pioneer but the question is "pioneer of what." On the other hand, the early days of cinema are filled with examples of films which we today perceive to be nothing more than recorded theatre plays. Positioned on the opposite pole from McLuhan and nowhere even close to Benjamin, those works are indicative of the shadow of the old medium in a new medium, old aesthetics disguised in new clothes.

The challenge I face as an artist using new technology is probably best summarised in the two above examples. The question I constantly ask myself is where I stand between the two poles of extremes.

You are also involved in the Swedish organisation Fylkingen. What kind of organisation is it?

Sachiko Hayashi: Fylkingen is a not-for-profit artist-run organisation in Stockholm. Established in 1933 as a chamber music society, it soon expanded its arena to include various intermedia art forms. Today its almost 80 years' history witnesses its dynamic drive to introduce and promote yet-to-be-established art forms in Sweden in a way there is no counterpart in the country. The examples of this include EAM (Electro-Acoustic Music) since the '50s, Video Art since the '70s (including the revival of Video Art in the '80s), Happenings in the '60s and Performance Art in the '70s, and Sound Art and Electronica in the '90s. As such, it has always served as the cutting-edge interface between Sweden and abroad. The names of the artists who have been introduced in Sweden by Fylkingen include Luciano Berio, Karlheinz Stockhausen, John Cage, Merce Cunningham, David Tudor, Nam June Paik, Shigeko Kubota, La Monte Young, Pauline Oliveros, and in recent years, Merzbow, Stelarc, etc. The list is almost literally endless.

The members of the organisation also reflect this unique status. The history of Fylkingen is highly entangled in the history of Swedish art history, as it has been a cradle and home for the country's leading composers, musicians, dancers, and pioneers of various fields (experimental cinema, experimental poetry in the form of text-sound composition, performance art, video art, sound art, improvised music, etc.), who pushed the boundaries in their respective fields.

Some notable examples are Bengt Hambraeus (EAM composer), Karl-Erik Welin (composer/pianist), Folke Rabe (composer), Åke Hodell (text-sound composer), Margareta Åsberg (dancer), Sten Hanson (text-sound composer/performance artist) and Carl Michael von Hausswolff (electronica/sound artist), to name only a few. Close associates include Måndagsgruppen (the most influential music association in Sweden in the '40s), Öyvind Fahlström, Pistol Teatern (experimental theatre which introduced happenings in Sweden in the '60s), Pontus Hultén and Moderna Muséet, Tekniska Muséet, Swedish Radio, etc. Fylkingen was also instrumental in bringing Elektronmusikstudion (EMS/Electronic Music Studio) in Stockholm into existence.

For Fylkingen you are editing the online *Hz-journal*. What is its focus?

Sachiko Hayashi: *Hz-journal*, published by Fylkingen, started as a non-online journal in the '90s by the initiative of Carl Michael von Hausswolff and Bo Rydberg. The intention was to replace and revive Fylkingen Bulletin, which emerged in 1966 as Fylkingen's journal for its members. In 2000 Hz was moved to the online platform by Kent Tandkred and Thomas Liljenberg. From 2003 I have been involved as a co-editor (Issue 2, with Thomas Liljenberg) and as the editor-in-chief (from Issue 3). From the Issue 3, the journal has been managed on the basis of international open calls and has become what Hz-journal is today. My intention with *Hz-journal* is that it be a journal for the practitioners of art forms that often fall outside traditional art categories. The journal is intended to serve as a forum for various non-traditional art practitioners to share thoughts and ideas that originate from the pursuit of non-traditional and non-conventional art practices.

This first priority is complemented with articles by theoreticians, critics, and curators, whose fields of main interest correspond to the above position. It is also my intention that *Hz-journal* as a journal with focus on "sharing" give room for in-depth texts by resisting reporting journalism, reviews, art criticism or texts with political intentions. As such, *Hz-journal* has been able to not only publish texts of a more philosophical nature but also reprint an MA thesis, a book chapter, as well as earlier published milestone texts, such as Kim Cascone's "The Aesthetics of Failure: 'Post-Digital' Tendencies in Contemporary Computer Music", Pauline Oliveros' "Quantum Improvisation: The Cybernetic Improvisation", and Roy Ascott's "Moistmedia, Technoetics and three VRs."

Togehether with HUMLab, you set up a Second Life residency program. Can you tell me about its background?

Sachiko Hayashi: Since 2010, HUMlab at Umeå University in Sweden and I have been running a virtual artist residency named Yoshikaze "Up-In-The-Air" Residency on HUMlab sim in Second Life (hereafter SL). HUMlab is a meeting place in RL (i.e. Real Life, as opposed to SL) for researchers and students at Umeå University, whose main purpose is to bring together various academic disciplines of humanities that involve new technology. HUMlab sim in Second Life, owned by HUMlab, consists of activities that reflect the RL HUMlab, including researches into virtual language-training, virtual religions, virtual museology, etc. Yoshikaze's artist residency is part of this SL HUMlab sim activity.

I am the curator of the programme and have been responsible for outlining the residency, selecting artists, and coordinating communications between our artists and HUMlab. PhD candidate at Umeå University James Barrett is the sim manager as well as the representative from HUMlab in the Yoshikaze management. At the end of each residency we offer a 5-day-long RL exhibition at HUMlab, for which HUMlab's art director Carl-Erik Engqvist also shares responsibility with Jim and me. All the financial decisions are taken by the HUMlab director Patrik Svensson.

The residency programme was born out of my experience of having been involved in Tagging Art's "Virtual Moves" project. In 2007 with the funding from the Danish Art Council, Tagging Art in Copenhagen selected 9 artists to make works of art in Second Life. I was one of the selected artists and found myself having to look for a virtual space for the purpose of building my work. This experience made me aware of the need of virtual studio space for artists in SL.

I became acquainted with HUMlab in 2006 when James Barrett and Patrik Svensson invited me to give a lecture. Upon my request, they also assisted me with availability of their virtual space in SL for my part in the Tagging Art's "Virtual Moves" exhibition at the National Gallery, Copenhagen, in 2008. Soon thereafter I managed to secure a part of HUMlab sim for the Second Life group Avatar Orchestra Metaverse (AOM), who was in need of a rehearsal location and of which I was a member at the time. When AOM a little later found another home in SL, the spot became redundant and inactive. Some time later with the agreement of the sim manager and the HUMlab director, I decided to reactivate the spot by experimenting with the idea of virtual residency.

What are the conditions for the residency program and how many artists have joined it so far?

Sachiko Hayashi: We are currently into our 7th resident artist, Pyewacket Kazyanenko, who, in addition to her own SL art practice, has assisted Stelarc in SL. Early this year we also had a special presentation by Kristine Schomaker about her two previous SL projects, both of which were made outside our residency program. If we include her presentation, Pyewacket Kazyanenko is our 8th artist to present her/his work at HUMlab.

The residency is purely virtual, i.e., the artist holds a residency within SL accessing our SL space from his/ her RL resident place. The residency is normally between 1-3 months; the length is usually chosen by the artist to best suit his/her project. The residency can be used to create a specific work of art or to explore a specific subject matter relevant to his/her art practice.

At the end of the residency, we provide a five day long RL show at HUMlab with the work(s) produced during the residency. At the opening of the show, we request the presence of the artist via the internet, either by Skype video or in SL, to give us an artist-talk or a presentation, alternatively an SL performance. The equipments available for our shows are seven fixed 57" screens, two fixed 63" screens, one fixed 70" screen, one portable 50" screen and one 63" portable screen; each of these monitors can be connected to computers. In addition, we use one super 176" multitouch screen for the presentation. During the course of residency, the artist is encouraged to document his/her progress on our blog and Vimeo sites.

Two aspects of the outer structure of the residency (blog and RL exhibition) are drawn from my involvement in the above-described Tagging Art project. The curators of Tagging Art, Annette Finnsdottir, Anne Holmfred, Iben Bentzen, and Ida Grøn, took many new challenges upon themselves for the "Virtual Moves" exhibition, among them documentation in the form of blog entries by each involved artist about the inner-working-process of building an artwork in a virtual sphere, and exploration of issues of RL display of SL art with involvement of general public uninitiated in the Second Life interface, the two issues which are seldom being addressed.

My criteria for selecting our artists have been 1) the artist has produced a significant body of work in Second Life and/or 2) the artist can carry out her/his project independently with his/her own set of inquiries in relation to his/her SL art practice. It has been my intention from the day one that the residency programme should not reflect my personal preference and taste; instead it be a place that shows diversity of perspectives that exist in the pursuit of SL/virtual art activities. Part of the strength of the Yoshikaze residency can be found in this un-authoritarian aesthetic neutrality, creating diverseness of residencies as well as their end results.

Do you like to mention some outcomes of the programme?

Sachiko Hayashi: Selavy Oh's *Construct*, which is a virtual installation consisting of 75 cubes, each of which she added to the construction on each day of her 75-day-long residency. Applying a different coding script to the content of each cube, the 75 cubes and their behind-the-scene-codings are containers of her residence days as in the form of a diary. *Construct* has received much attention, attracting comments, interviews, and articles about the work, amongst which was a presentation of the work by Lori Landay at the MIT conference Media in Transition 7.

Juria Yoshikawa, a.k.a. Lance Sheilds and Garrett Lynch each explored the parallel worlds of existence between RL and SL. Prior to enrolling in the Yoshikaze residency, Lance Shields as the female avatar Juria Yoshikawa has actively produced large-scale immersive installations that surround visiting avatars. His work for the residency would depart from that history by integrating the elements of his daily life around the issue of son-father relationship into Juria's work. Though unfinished due to his workload in RL, this work, presented by his SL female persona Juria as her creation, would have created an intriguing sphere of interchange and discord between his real and virtual life.

The interplay of correspondence/dis-correspondence between the two worlds was also the focus of Garrett Lynch. With identity and place as his central theme, Garrett investigated into our notion of "real," by placing his avatar and his dual self Garrett Lynch (IRL) in various places and sceneries, at times by stretching SL's boundary into Google Earth and at other times by building augmented reality devices for his avatar in SL. He finished his residency with a technically advanced mixed-reality performance, incorporating both elements of visual and audio as real-time mixed-reality components (as opposed to the more common form of real-time audio mixed-reality) with access via Second Life (as opposed to access in RL, which is more commonly done).

For me personally, the most memorable artist-in-residence in our two-year-history has been Katerina Karoussos, who, during her two-and-half-months' residency at Yoshikaze, conducted a methodical step-by-step inquiry into our understanding (noesis) of the virtual. As part of her PhD research at Planetary Collegium, her residency was never about producing work of art for a show case but an opportunity to delve into the depth of her theme, the findings of which she shared in the form of blog entries, vimeo documentations, and a presentation. She engaged the benefits of her time as our artist-in-residence in the way no other form than a residency would have been able to provide. In that sense, she stood out and still stands out in her uniqueness.

Why is SL so interesting for artists? What does it offer that no other virtual world can offer?

Sachiko Hayashi: Answering your first question "Why is SL so interesting for artists?" I do not have a general answer to that. Artists in SL come from diverse backgrounds, just as netart or other forms of New Media, bringing various perspectives onto the table, which makes generalisation risky to make. Even the term "virtual" can be investigated from several different angles, as in defiance of reality (Alan Sondheim, Fau Ferdinand, Pyewacket Kazyanenko), reality embedded in coding (Selavy Oh), expanding reality (Garrett Lynch), metaphysics (Katerina Karoussos) and identity (Kristine Schomaker), to name examples from the works by the artists we've had at Yoshikaze.

Speaking solely from my own experience, though I do not consider myself a SL artist and most of my current activities fall outside SL, three engaging SL characteristics can be mentioned as below:

1) SL's "blank canvas" (that is to say metaphorically), which offers no pre-determined rules to follow. SL differs from online games in the aspect there is no game to play. Combined with it are SL's internal 3D authoring tool and scripting language which enable creation and modification of one's objects and environment, making SL an independent desktop with its own authoring tools. It is a common practice for SL artists to combine this freedom with SL's built-in virtual features that disengage physical laws, such as flying and transportation (annulment of gravity) and walk-through/touch-through and deformation of objects (collapse of atoms), etc., all of which is considered to be a sign of virtuality in its opposition to what is natural and real in our physical world.

2) SL's networked space, which denies geographical limitation. For example aforementioned Avatar Orchestra Metaverse (AOM) is a group of composers and musicians who acknowledge this environment as a crucial component of their collaborative creativity. Except for two geographical pockets (Regensburg in Germany and Vancouver/Victoria in British Columbia of Canada), the people involved in the group live far away from each other; the members are spread over 8 different countries, including all the different time zones in USA, and most of them have never met the other members in RL. Despite this circumstance, they compose together, build their own virtual instruments together, rehearse together and give concerts in SL regularly.

3) SL's use of avatar, who becomes the artist who paints SL's "blank canvas." A work of art in Second Life is created via the use of an avatar, an approach that distinguishes SL from external 3D authoring tools. Although SL can support external files for animation, avatar formation, etc., the files have to be uploaded to SL to be integrated by an avatar. This mode of self-representation presents a unique juncture which both merges and dissociates artist/the creator in RL and avatar/the creator in SL.

In some artists this conjuncture manifests in gender bending (Gazira Babeli, SaveMe Oh, Selavy Oh, Juria Yoshikawa, Pyewacket Kazyanenko) which draws a clear line between oneself and one's artist persona as in roleplaying, whereas in others (Garrett Lynch and Kristine Schomaker) this dualism has been made into their central theme. My latest work *Experimentation #1*, a RL audio-visual performance integrating SL in part, also partially addresses this issue.

First published on *Digicult* in June 2012 with the title "Up in the Air with Sachiko Ayashi".

Krystian Majewski

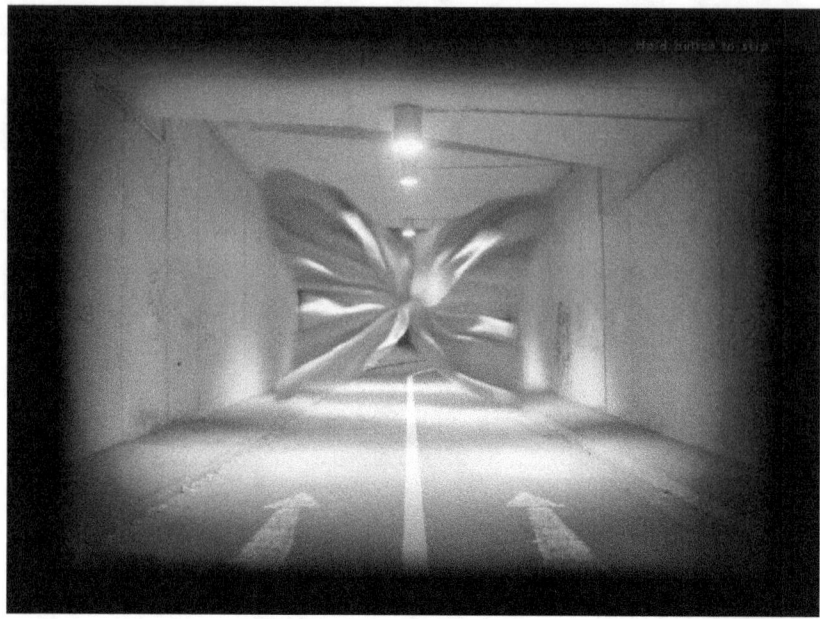

Krystian Majewski, *TRAUMA*, 2011. Screenshot

Krystian Majewski (http://kisd.de/~krystian/) was born in 1981 in Warsaw, Poland but grew up in Darmstadt, Germany. He studied design at the Köln International School of Design while working as a freelancer for various clients. Together with Yu-Chung Chen and Daniel Renkel he runs a collaborative game design network named Creative Units (CEEU) and the two blogs *Game Design Reviews* and *Game Design Scrapbook*.

Majewski has made an impact on the indie game scene with his innovative photographic adventure game *TRAUMA* (2011), about a young woman who survives a car accident. Recovered at the hospital, she has dreams that shed light on different aspects of her identity – like the way she deals with the loss of her parents. The game is a deep game for a mature audience, that has recently won the German Game Award as the best browser game.

Mathias Jansson: What inspires you?

Krystian Majewski: Ideas can come from everywhere. I think the trick is to maintain a steady stream of input from fresh sources. Especially game developers seem to be very focused on Sci-Fi and Fantasy themes nowadays. So as a game developer, I think it's important to dig into other topics as well in order to avoid locking yourself in. The inspirations for *TRAUMA* came from various trends in photography. Essays about modern architecture and how space is being processed by the human mind. There were some more intimate, biographical influences as well.

You mention *TRAUMA*, can you tell me more about it?

Krystian Majewski: *TRAUMA* was really a long journey. I started out with the goal of creating a modernized adventure game. By doing some research it occurred to me that adventure games have continually evolved to become more and more accessible. Early text adventures were incredibly unforgiving and obscure. It was a revolution back in the days when Lucasarts started developing adventures where you couldn't die, or when Cyan got rid of all the verbs in Myst. Especially Cyan realized that by going this route, it's possible to address a completely different audience.

TRAUMA is an extrapolation of many such patterns. What if an adventure game wouldn't be even about puzzles and challenges? What if an adventure game would be very short so you can play it in one evening? What it if an adventure game would tackle more serious and mature topics?

I feel like there is some great untapped potential along this line of thinking. Some more recent releases like Dear Esther, Dinner Date or To The Moon seem to be echoing this sentiment.

Besides creating games you are also running a blog called *Game Design Reviews*. Can you tell me the idea behind the blog and what do you think makes a good game design?

Krystian Majewski: Game Design Reviews and Game Design Scrapbook are both places for me to just collect various thoughts, ideas and observations. I think having a place like this is very important for every game designer. And it's not just about recording and remembering. It's often during the process of writing when all the ideas develop properly for the first time. And of course, being able to discuss them with fellow designers and gamers is essential too.

In the end, it's not really possible to define what a good game is. It really depends on what you are trying to do. You need a wide palette of tools to chose from so you always have the right one ready when the need arises.

What do you think about the current German indie game scene?

Krystian Majewski: I'm a bit disappointed with the current state of the German indie game scene. There are not many of us and most of the games are simple, small-minded and visually unremarkable. Recently, there have been some new developments. There are some new funding opportunities and some new schools. I have been helping out with local Global Game Jams for the last 3 years and I observed an astonishing growth there. I sense that there may be a long-needed storm brewing.

Finally do you have any advice to give to someone that is thinking of working as an indie game designer in the future? What kind of education and skills does she need to succeed in this hard branch?

Krystian Majewski: I'm going to be controversial by saying: don't become a programmer. Of course, you NEED to know how to program but that's something you can learn on your own. It's not that hard, it just takes time and practice. The thing that's really hard to do is to design. How to come up with ideas? How to develop them? How to communicate them properly? Jonathan Blow once made this presentation called »Programming is Easy; Production is Harder; Design is Hardest«. And he started out as a programmer.

Otherwise, find something that makes you unique. Something a big company can't do. Something that makes people go "wow, I have never seen anything like it". And then just go with it as far as you can.

First published in *Next-level* in May 2012 with the title "Interview with Krystian Majewski creator of TRAUMA".

Christy Matson and Melissa Baron

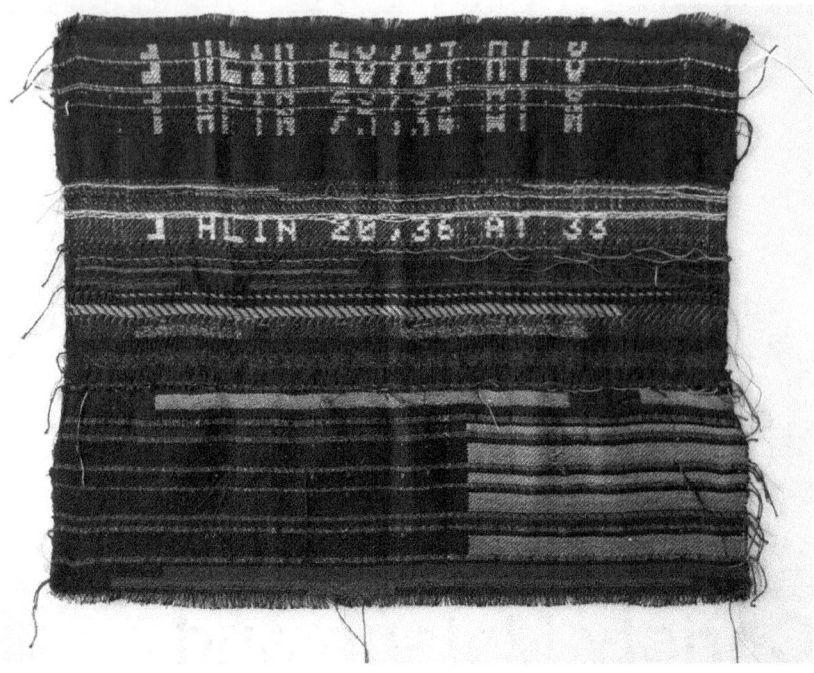

Melissa Barron, *Jacquard Weavings*, 2010. Image courtesy the artist.

Christy Matson (http://cmatson.com/) and Melissa Barron (http://melissabarron.net/) are two artists that combine digital video games with weaving. In their art they explore the borders between virtual and real images, but also the close relationship between early computer history and the tradition of handicraft.

At the beginning of the XIX century, the French manufacturer Joseph Jaquard invented a mechanical loom that could weave complex patterns with the help of punch cards. The idea with punch cards was later adapted and used to program computers, so you could say that computer technology was developed thanks to the wish to mechanize handicraft products. Both Matson and Barron are using the Jaquard loom in their art to weave patterns found in the digital realm. Matson grabbed landscapes from the video game Loom (1990) and Barron made weavings from different crack screens found in Apple II games.

The term "Craft Hackers" is an appropriate description of Matson's and Barron's art. The term was first used in a panel discussion held at the New

Museum in December 2008, with a reference to "artists who use crafting techniques to explore high-tech culture and the relationship between needlework and computer programming." Beside Christy Matson, the panel included Ben Fino-Radin, who translates the World Wide Web into needlepoint sculptures of yarn and plastic; Cody Trepte, whose embroidery reminds of retired computer punch cards; and Cat Mazza, who knits moving images in yarn.

Mathias Jansson: Christy, what's your relationship with video games?

Christy Matson: I don't play video games, so I have almost no relationship at all to them. When I was a child, we had an Atari and I remember playing Pac Man on it. I think my brother broke it after a couple of months though. I was in elementary school when the first Nintendos came out and I recall being the only kid in my class whose parent's wouldn't buy them one. I played games like Super Mario Bros often when I would go to other kid's houses. We had computer games as a child though, I would spend hours playing games like Oregon Trail, Where in the World in Carmen San Diego and King's Quest. King Quest is probably most similar to Loom in the structure of the game and how you progress through it. A former student turned me onto the game Loom after hearing me lecture about my work. I learned to play the game just so that I could capture all of the screen shots out of it. The game is from the early 90's so in many ways it is reminiscent of the style of games that I would play as a child in the 80's.

Melissa, when did you fall in love with old Apple games?

Melissa Barron: My first experience with the Apple 2 computer was in elementary school in the mid 90s. I played a lot of the MECC games such as Number Munchers, Spellevator, Odell Lake, and The Oregon Trail. I didn't have a computer at home, so I only played the games that were available at school. I remember being intrigued by the Apple 2 at that age, but I was never allowed to do anything more with it besides play games. It would have been fun to learn how to program and make my own games, but we were never given the option. At that time I didn't even know that the Commodore 64 and Atari systems existed. After I left elementary school I forgot about the Apple 2 and it wasn't until recently (2009) that I realized that emulators existed and rediscovered a lot of the old games I used to play. I've since acquired actual hardware and now try to do a lot of things I never was able to do when I was younger, such as programming.

Christy, your experience with the adventure game Loom (Lucasfilms Games,1990) resulted in the project *Loomscapes* (2008). Can you tell me why you choose that game?

Christy Matson: I knew I wanted to use the game Loom as source material for a project. I had been combining sound and hand-weaving for a number of years so this game was right up my alley. Up to this point, I had mainly been using the Jacquard loom to weave abstract imagery, but this felt like the perfect opportunity to combine weaving and representational imagery. I liked that while referencing landscapes, the images were fantastical, surreal and invented. I used the horizontal format for the weavings because it referenced both the tradition of narrative storytelling via tapestry weaving (Bayeux Tapestry for example) as well as the format for how the game is laid out (i.e. when the protagonist, Bobbin Threadbare walks off the screen to the left, the entire landscape changes frame by frame.)

The Jacquard seemed a great output method for these pieces too because of its historical connections to the early computing technology. In fact, in the game Loom, there is a "great loom" that more or less reigns over what's left of the planet (the game takes place in the future, in a post-apocalyptic environment. the Earth has been destroyed by technology and the only survivors are crafts-people: Weavers, Blacksmiths, and Shepherds.) The landscapes are actually beautiful when woven. I used a cotton yarn together with a stainless steel yarn. The pieces were washed after I made them and the cotton shrank in a way that the stainless steel did not. The surface of the pieces is actually quite dimensional and tactile. Although the pieces are presented flat and stretched, they had a 3D surface quality to them that I think contrasts nicely with the flat quality of the screen in the game.

Melissa, you also work with the Jacquard Loom. In your Apple 2 crack screens woven on a tc-1 jacquard loom, you used crack screens, that is the intro crackers made to show the world who had cracked the copyright protection of the game. Why?

Melissa Barron: The connection between the Jacquard loom and the first computer was the main reason why I started working on the loom. I wanted to see what I could do with the machine and definitely wanted to try and glitch it. What I found exciting about the loom was that fact that the machine wasn't completely computerized, it still required the user to stand at the loom and pass the shuttle (the device that holds the thread) back and forth. This added another chance of possible mistakes/errors that I would unintentionally make myself, which I often did.

Melissa, you mention you tried to "glitch" the Loom. What kind of glitches are you looking for in your art?

Melissa Barron: When I'm working with the Apple 2 emulator, most of the time I'll just open a disk image in a text editor and then take out or add various bits in different places. I've noticed patterns in disk images where I know it will create something interesting and then try to avoid the places I know would just break the disk entirely. I'll then usually transfer it to a floppy disk to see it work on the hardware. When I want to work on the actual hardware, I'll usually open the software in a sector editor and play around with that. It's more difficult that way, but I've never been afraid of doing things the hard way. I don't really look for any particular type of glitch, I mainly just work until I find something beautiful.

Although, I do like being able to see fragments of the original source. With the weavings, I didn't just want to weave screen captures of glitches. I wanted to weave images that I could glitch while utilizing different functions of the loom and various weave structures. I wanted the loom to create the glitches. The outcome was a bit more unexpected and it created pieces that are incredibly fragile that continue to deteriorate as they are handled more.

Christy, you have returned to the game Loom in one of you later works, _Future Positive_ (2011). In this case there is a looser relationships between the virtual game world and the real installation...

Christy Matson: In _Future Positive_ we (also a collaboration with Jon and Sarah) were only referencing the video game very, very loosely. We weren't really interested in making super direct or overt relationships between the game and the work in the show but it was used as a starting point for building the narrative around each of the three vignettes in the show.

We decided to use the structure of the video game to create three-tiered "levels" (environments / kits / etc) with the idea that the three installations would be in order with the first one being plant based, the second one with conductive sheep, and the third inspired by a lightning storm.

At this point there is no direct correlation between the actual game and the 3 different pieces in the show but we do feel there are numerous relationships between materials (cloth, rocks, metal wires, paper), representational imagery (shoes, rugs, sheeps and flower sculptures) and phenomenology (lighting, sound, implied narratives from the titles, etc) which are rich with possibilities such that the entire show might lay bare an elemental vocabulary through which viewers might reconstruct any number of narratives.

One of the pieces on display, *Twin Flowers + Magnetize Money Spell Kit*, is a floor-to-ceiling walk-through environment with electro-acoustic solar-powered flora hanging over a ball-point-pen-plotted rendering of Jeff the "Dude" Lebowski's famous "soiled" carpet. A second piece titled *6 Minutes to Diamond Consciousness* has two sculptural sheeps that conduct six volts of electric power as they engage in psychic warfare with a large-scale two-dimensional rendering.

The third piece *Star Doves Smoky Mountain Light* is comprised primarily of an animal form immersed in flashes of projected and reflected light of questionable intent. So while the game functioned as a starting point, the working process was much looser and the work became something else all together.

You both mention the importance of the MECC game Oregon Trail, an educational game about the 19th century pioneer life on the Oregon Trail. The game was first release in 1971, and since then have been re-published many times. Melissa, you spent hours to translate the game into L337, chatspeak and LOLcats grammar. The final work is called *73H 0r3g0n 7r41L* (2009). Why did you choose Oregon Trail?

Melissa Barron: Oregon Trail was a popular and iconic game for a lot of people of my age. Because of this I didn't really want to change the story line all that much but update it for a newer generation that never played the original game. I enjoy combining the old with the new in order to create something completely different. Changing the text also makes it harder to play the game and it almost becomes another game trying to decipher it if you aren't familiar with the language. Also, considering that it was an educational game it makes it even funnier to me.

So, how did you create *73H 0r3g0n 7r41L*?

Melissa Barron:The creation of *73H 0r3g0n 7r41L* was a simple but long process. I was reminded of the game after hearing about a newer version being released on the iPhone, and after a quick search I found the disk images and an Apple 2 emulator to play the original game that I remembered. I tried opening the disk images in a text editor (TextEdit for Mac) and amongst the mess of ascii characters, I recognized text strings from the game. I then changed a couple of those characters just to see what would happen. It worked and from there I proceeded to change every character in the game. Bit by bit. This was the only way I knew how to do it at that time.

It took months as you can imagine. The hardest part was that I had to preserve the original byte count. If I added one too many characters or left one out, it would break the game. As you can imagine I made a lot of mistakes but sometimes they created really interesting glitches. The video, *Error 107 at line #312* (2010) is a screen capture of my very first glitch. The various glitches that occurred during *73H 0r3g0n 7r41L* process were the inspiration for some of my later glitch weavings.

First published in *Digimag*, issue 68, October 2011 with the title "Craft Hacking in the Loom: Interview with Christy Matson and Melissa Baron".

Iman Moradi and
Max Capacity

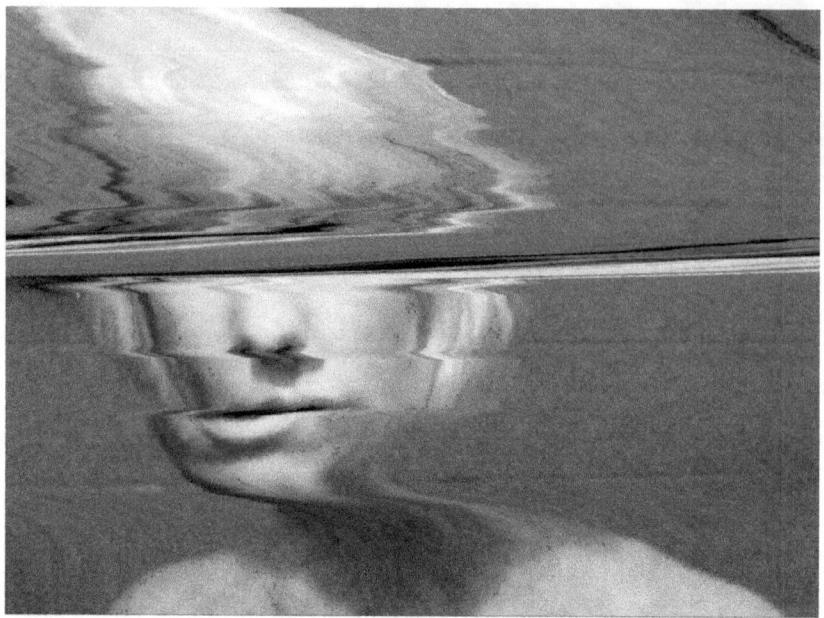

Rosa Menkman, *A Vernacular of File Formats – Bitmap File (.BMP). Windows 24bit (irreversible databend)*, 2011. Digital print on Dbond, 30 x 40 cm. Image courtesy Fabio Paris Art Gallery.

For a young artist, Marcel Duchamp's famous painting *Nude Descending a Staircase, No. 2* (1912) may look like an early example of glitch art. When Duchamp made the painting, he recorded the movement of the woman walking down the stairs: a similar visual effect can be now experienced when you have a corrupt graphic card which is not erasing the traces from the moving object on the screen.

Duchamp's work, of course, has more to do with Eadweard Muybridge's photographic studies of motion, and with the concerns of the Futurist movement, its fascination for new technologies and for the aesthetics of speed.

Since then, technology has always fascinated artists, but there is also a backside of the coin. Not even in the most advanced futuristic illusion technology is perfect. In a well known scene from *The Matrix* (1999), the main character Neo experiences what he describes as a déjà vu, a cat walking twice over the floor. Trinity explains the experience to Neo. "A deja vu is usually a glitch in the Matrix. It happens when they change something." Glitches in computer systems create unexpected events, and for the common user malfunction or failure in software or hardware often causes frustration and anger.

But for a new generation of artists these bugs, errors and glitches are source for artistic expression. Glitches could be described as secrets doors to the system, like when Neo in *The Matrix* sees behind the interface and discovers that it's built of 0s and 1s, thus realizing that it can be manipulated and modified. In the same way glitch artists are trying to manipulate the system or looking for weaknesses in the system to go beyond the "perfect" interface.

Iman Moradi, Senior Lecturer at the University of Huddersfield, is one of the leading theorist of Glitch Art, and the editor (with Ant Scott, Joe Gilmore & Christopher Murphy) of one of the first books on the subject: *Glitch: Designing Imperfection* (Mark Batty Publisher, New York 2009).

Mathias Jansson: Iman, when did glitch art start?

Iman Moradi: Tricky to ask this question about when Glitch Art was started or indeed arrived at a clever, all encompassing definition of Glitch Art itself. I think at the point where an artist called the "unexpected" the result of a mistranslation, or indeed the provocation of a medium, to produce unexpected results, art became Glitch art. For me it was when I discovered Ant Scott's (Beflix) work back in the summer of 2001. For me he legitimized what I thought was pretty cool to begin with and called it Glitch Art. He basically curated found and generated examples of visual glitches on his blog. They were very tasteful and had an air of humor and emotion about them. I personally started to explore it within an academic context at the first available opportunity that I had in 2003 - 2004 and got in touch with Ant Scott. The Oslo Glitch Symposium in 2002 was I believe, the first formal point where glitch art was being discussed.

In your PHD thesis *Glitch Aesthetics* (2004) you categorize glitch-art into pure-glitches and glitch-alike. What is the difference between these two categories?

Iman Moradi: I get a bit of flak these days for making that categorization and perhaps, rightly so. I stipulated that Glitches that are naturally discovered and found are somehow more pure, and the ones that are faked – for example if you paint or draw a glitch, or design a likeness of it, or create a glitch effect using a plugin, would be a glitch-alike. Sometimes categorization helps us understand, or divert unnecessary commentary. One of the questions and comments I used to get very bored with was: its not a glitch if its provoked. Being a visual designer and producer myself, I like to have control over all aspects of what I produce, and aside from the sometime pleasant and unexpected visual surprises I want to roughly know how to achieve a particular effect. For me most glitches that are used in an art context are Glitch-alikes, they are really representations of aspects of glitches framed as art or used within other design contexts for their sheer visual qualities.

Why are so many glitch artist interested in working with old software and hardware?

Iman Moradi: Technology of old used to be more susceptible to being in a state of glitch, and the trend in consumer electronics is for things to NOT glitch at all, the future is always going to be higher fidelity and higher signal clarity where possible to eliminate all glitches, which is kind of uninteresting. So, as far as old technology and glitches go, I think they two go hand in hand. You have people like Jeff Donaldson, of Notendo fame who modify hardware for the specific purpose of generating glitch visuals for use in performance contexts. The glitch is also for me inextricably linked with a sense of nostalgia and longing for how things used to be, in that they were imperfect! There's a lot of character and interest in things that are imperfect; it humanizes technology and somehow makes it more human and flawed, like ourselves.

Is there any special genre in glitch-art dealing with video-games and glitches?

Iman Moradi: None, that I'm personally that acquainted with and maybe there should be. If its just glitches from games captured by gamers, would you call it art or something else? I do actually get annoyed with the saturation of game related glitch stuff when you search for glitch on the likes of Youtube. As far as the relationship of glitch-art to glitches goes, there are undoubtedly elements of the glitch aesthetic that borrow heavily from the glitching that some games used to exhibit with dodgy display drivers and such. I'd say Nullpointer's (Tom Betts) QQQ, was a the first example I saw, of using a particular glitch effect in a modded game which I absolutely loved.

In your thesis you compared glitch art with modernist painting, with references to Juan Gris, Gerhard Richter etc. Could you

say that Cubism, Constructivism etc. are result of errors or mistakes during the painting process?

Iman Moradi: I wouldn't say errors at all. I think initially I was purely looking at finding parallels in the visual qualities, linearity, fragmentation and perhaps complexity and of course aspects of style and composition that were similar. I was basically saying that our appreciation of the visual forms and sometimes the conceptual forms, are rooted in our prior willingness to accept and our appreciation of those established styles and movements.

What about glitch art and the contemporary art scene? Does it have a position in the New Media Art landscape?

Iman Moradi: You only need to look at the fantastic efforts of Jon Satrom, Evan Meaney, Jon Cates, Rosa Menkman, Nick Briz, and other organisers and presenters of the Gli.tc/h Event (symposium, conference, festival, about noise & new media) to see that the glitch is here to stay and firmly embedded in the new media art scene. I think the book *Glitch: Designing Imperfection*, I jointly edited and which was published by MBP New York in 2009 also shows that the glitch has entered a level of recognition that goes beyond enthusiasts or mere hobbyists, it's firmly rooted in academia, popular culture and contemporary artistic endeavor.

Max Capacity, currently living in Santa Cruz, California, is an artist and illustrator often concerned with retro-style graphics, pixels and glitches. His work is well represented on Flickr and Tumblr. Max, when did you realize that you could use glitches as a medium for aesthetic expression?

Max Capacity: I only realized earlier this year that people cared about glitches as much as I do. I was on Flickr and I had uploaded some glitches I captured and I found there were a bunch of glitch-related groups and lots of glitch art already posted across Flickr. I had no idea. I've been doing this stuff at home in my garage or bedroom for a while, but I didn't think anyone else cared.

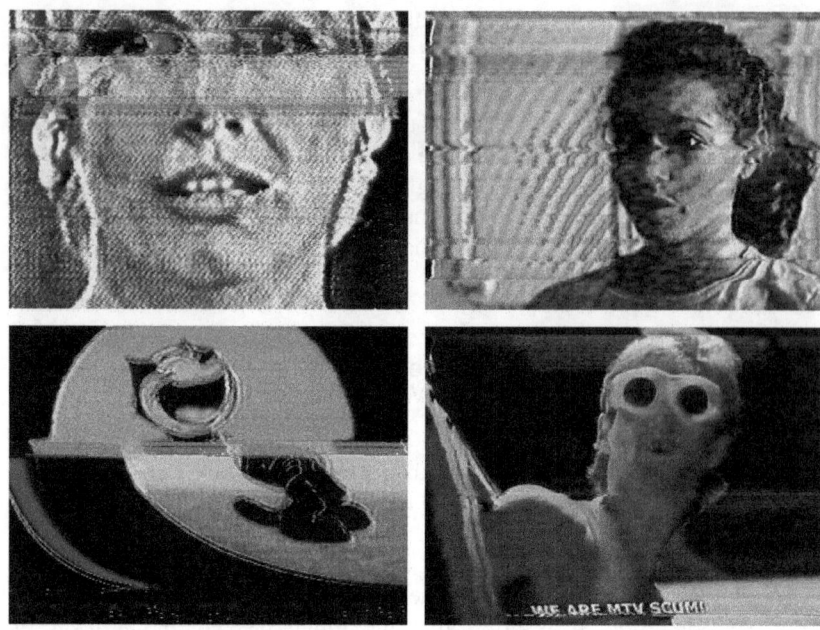

Max Capacity, from the series *Analog Video Glitch*, 2011. Images courtesy the artist.

What are you looking for when you create your glitch art?

Max Capacity: I really appreciate hardware glitches. I remember trying to watch scrambled pornography on cable TV when I was young. And I remember my frustration with my NES system when a cartridge would glitch out and I'd lose my game. Now that I don't care so much, I can just appreciate the beauty. I think there's a certain sort of nihilism and entropy present in glitch art that I think is relevant these days. Decay can be beautiful in it's own way.

Is there any particular category of games or programs that is more interesting for you to use?

Max Capacity: I'll glitch almost any game these days, but I always come back to the NES. I'd love to get into some arcade games and circuit bend them a little. But the NES is so accessible. Besides the availability of old NES hardware, there's also lots of great technical info homebrew hardware and emulators on the internet. I definitely lean towards NES games attached to movie franchises, or ports of arcade games.

Glitch theorist Iman Moradi distinguishes between two categories of glitches: the pure glitch, that is "the result of a malfunction or error"; and the glitch-alike, that happens when the artist creates the environment that is required to invoke a glitch and anticipate one to happen. What do you think about this?

Max Capacity: At first all my glitches were accidental and I thought they were worth capturing. But I quickly got tired of waiting for them to happen and started to make them myself. I think it's easy for me because most of the stuff I use is already half-broken. And I don't take good care of my electronics. So the difference between a cable accidentally being plugged into the wrong place, or purposefully being plugged into the wrong place is mostly academic to me. The accidental glitches are a great place for me to start experimenting from. The good part about it is that I used to try to make things work and I'd be frustrated that they didn't work. Now I try to figure out new and novel ways to make things break. It satisfies my appetite for destruction and my creative drive at the same time.

How do you experience glitch art on the contemporary art scene?

Max Capacity: I don't really experience glitch art in the world much at all except what I see on Flickr or Tumblr. I mostly stay at home and play with my electronics and computers. Like I was saying earlier, I didn't even know glitch art was popular with anyone besides me. I think glitch art fits in under the umbrella of avant-garde. And probably similar to lots of historical movements like cubism. I try not to think about that too much. I love looking at all the glitch art on the internet, that always gets me excited. I get a lot of inspiration from video art from the 70's and 80's. But I think it was the scrambled pornography and glitched Nintendo cartridges that really made me do it.

First published on *Digimag*, Issue 61, February 2011, with the tittle "The fine art of glitches cheats and errors".

Shinji Murakami

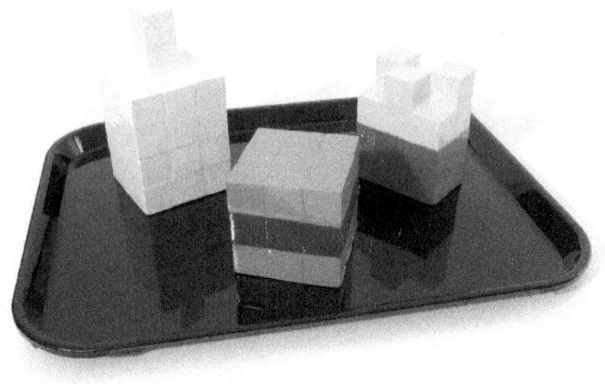

Shinji Murakami, *Happy Meal*, 2011. Wood blocks, glue, acrylic, resin, screw and plastic tray, 5.5 x 13.5 x 10.5 in. Image courtesy the artist.

When the US video game industry crashed in 1983, it was the beginning of the golden age of Japanese video games, with companies as Nintendo and Sega. During this period, top-star game designers like Shigeru Miyamoto created legendary video games such as Super Mario, Donkey Kong and The Legend of Zelda. Later on, the role-playing games (RPG) genre took a big jump when Hironobu Sakaguchi presented the successful RPG series Final Fantasy in 1987.

With such an historical background, you may think that Japan, as USA and Europe, have a strong tradition of contemporary artists inspired by video games, with regular Game Art exhibitions in the country. After all, Japan is the promised land of popular culture. Surprisingly enough, this isn't happening. An exception is Japanese artist Shinji Murakami (www.snz-e.com), born in 1980 in Osaka and grown up "on a healthy diet of classic 8-bit video-games", with The Legend of Zelda as a favourite.

Recently, a strong retro-trend and interest in the old 8-bit graphics developed in the art world, as well as in other fields of culture. In music, composers such as Nullsleep, Bitshifter and Goto80 are experimenting with chip music; in the indie game scene, 8-bit style games are a common trend, and famous game creators such as Cactus, Mark Essen and Jason Rohrer are contributing to it. Furthermore, object and fashion designers borrow elements from old arcade games and characters. An explanation to this retro-trend is that the computer generation has grown up and is looking back to the aesthetics of its childhood games for inspiration.

In the art field, artists are inspired by the classic 8-bit video games aesthetics in various ways. I call this trend "Neoarcadism". What are Neoarcadism's defining characters? It is art inspired by 8-bits graphics, which tries to emulate this ancient graphic expression, both in digital and analogue art objects. The objects are often built with the help of squares in different colours, making the picture look edgy as low resolution graphics. Neoarcadism can be also seen as a reaction to today's computer graphics, that try to be hyper-realistic and imitate reality as much as possible. You can find a parallel in the history of art. When photography was introduced in the XIX century, suddenly there was a medium able to portray reality accurately, and painters found it difficult to compete with photography's detailed realism in portraits and landscape paintings. So, they began to explore alternative ways of representing reality. In the same way, Neoarcadism could be seen as a reaction to the current pursuit of photo-realism in graphics, but also as a nostalgic look back to the history of video games.

Another important thing in Neoarcadism is the close relationship to handicraft. These artists are often interested in traditional art forms as mosaics, sculptures, paintings, or in the case of Murakami, stamps on wooden blocks or silkscreen print. They get inspiration from video games but transfers the digital image onto traditional art objects where you can find traces of the artists' hand. French street artist Space Invader is a good example: he makes small mosaics of famous 8-bit characters from games like Space Invaders and Pac-Man. These handmade mosaics are placed around the world in different cities. More recently, he also started making sculptures with the help of Rubik's cubes. Each cube could be used as 3x3 pixel grid with 6 different colours.

Another example is the Swedish artist Kristoffer Zetterstrand, who in his paintings makes a mash up of art history and classic arcade games, emulating the typical 8-bit feel in his paintings. Zetterstrand also made several public mosaics inspired by arcade games. For obvious reasons, mosaic is very popular in Neoarcadism, as artists like Norbert Bayer aka Mr.Ministeck, Benjamin Teck, and Arno Coenen show. Mosaic reminds how 8-bit graphics wered done in the beginning.

I talked about these issues with Shinji Murakami.

Mathias Jansson: What's so fascinating in 8-bit graphics? What kind of games inspires you?

Shinji Murakami: I love the simple expressions, and minimalism in games. Other important thing is the nostalgia, because I was crazy about Nintendo (NES and Super NES) when I was a kid. I think it's amazing that Nintendo's famous 8-bit characters could express so much with only 16x16 pixels! And how they created these very large worlds recycling limited materials in each game is also fascinating. The kind of games that inspire me the most are role-playing games and side-view action games, especially role-playing games like the first Zelda.

You started as a street artist and used to tag cities with your 8-bit characters Boco and Kid Snz. Can you tell me something about these characters?

Shinji Murakami: Yes, I started as a street artist, by putting stones in the streets which I painted and tagged. I couldn't tag on the walls at first, because I was very afraid of being arrested. I don't like the writers who tag names that sound like English, I mean most Japanese can't speak English well. I also felt a sense of incongruity in working with the European or American style. So I began tagging the image of the sword and the shield, those images are inspired from stereotype items from RPGs. Then, I drew a lot of characters to find my favourite ones as my new tags. A girlfriend of mine chose one of them. I obeyed her choice, because I believe in her intuition, and the character was "Kawaii" ("cute" in Japanese). That's the original Boco. Boco's concept is a simple drawing which looks like a kid's drawing. I mean, a kid's drawing with a minimum of expression, like 8-bit graphic is a minimum of a bitmap image. And I think that Kid Snz expresses most out of a minimum bitmap graphic, with only 9x7 pixels.

What do you think about street art as an illegal act?

Shinji Murakami: My opinion about street art is contradictory. Did you see my street work that bombed the billboard? I put the logo of NIKE or NISSAN on the same place with my drawing. In this case, I tried an experiment, so that people would recognize those billboards show true advertisement by putting a logo. One more thing: though it is an illegal act, some gallery owners such as Jeffrey Deitch really like it, and a market is formed. I just think that the street is going to be unimaginative if street art disappears.

In a series called RPG you have worked with maps, for example you have created a map over Central Park in New York in Final Quest 1 style. Can you tell me how this RGP maps are created and why did you choose to work with a style that reminds traditional Japanese art?

Shinji Murakami: "If I made a tree icon and put a lot of them next to each other, I'd be able to make a forest map!" This was the little light bulb of an idea that started my map artwork in 2003. I put my original stamps with images of "Map data" and "Item data" on a wood panel with a white painted background. I drew the "Character data" with a marker. I used to make only small works, because the rooms are small in Japan. So the stamp was matched for the method to repeat the image for that size. The surface of the canvas had small irregularities, so I used the wood panel that is more flat than canvas. I am not conscious that my work could remind of a particularly Japanese old style. In fact, after I moved to New York, I used silk-screening to make bigger sizes.

In your latest work you started to explore 3D-8bit. What brought you from 2D to 3D?

Shinji Murakami: Yes, I'm trying to explore the art of 3D-8bit. In Japan in 2005, there was a joint marketing campaign between Pepsi and Nintendo gaining recognition for its production of a 3D-8bit version of Super Mario Bros. Japan has a big Otaku culture today, so a lot of new figures (it means like a toy doll) are always released, but this product excited me and was very inspiring. I always want to discover new styles, and I was interested in making a sculpture in a new style. As an artist that has continued to utilize 8-bit games as a motif in his artwork, I felt compelled to create my own 3D-8bit artwork, and in 2009, I completed *Fruits Bowl*.

Can you tell me something about the Japanese Game Art scene? Are there many contemporary artists inspired by video games in Japan today? Are museums and galleries interested in displaying this kind of art?

Shinji Murakami: First, it's worth noting that there is almost no market for contemporary art in Japan today, and there is almost no culture of purchasing art. This is one of the reasons why I moved to New York. In fact, people in Japan don't understand why the Japanese artist Takashi Murakami is famous in the world, and they are not curious about it. There are a lot of art museums and galleries in Japan, but they seem to be a place for the elderly to entertain themselves. Some galleries ask money to the artists to loan their space. Is this an attractive art scene? There are a lot of artists who use motifs from Manga or Anime in the tradition of Takashi Murakami, but there is little interest in video games. Maybe I'm prejudiced, but the answer to this question is: no!

First published on *Digimag*, Issue 58, October 2010 with the title "Back to the Square: Shinji Murakami and Neoarcadism".

Jason Nelson

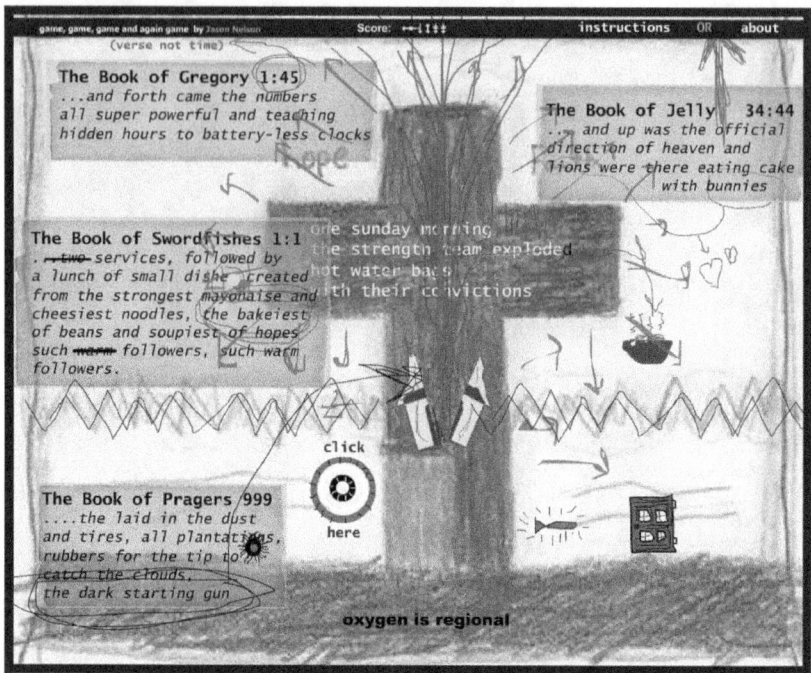

Jason Nelson, *Game, Game, Game and Again Game*, 2010. Online game, screenshot.

On the screen I can see some soldiers debarking a vessel; wading ashore between wooden barriers during constant gunfire. A voice is mimicking the sounds of gun shots and explosions. What I am looking at is *Emerging Poetry and video games* (2009), a one minute video by Carlos González Tardón, a Spanish researcher focused on immersion in video games, artificial intelligence and robotics. [1]

The video is a machinima, a video recorded with the help of a video game – in this case, one of the countless commercial war games you could find in every game shop. The machinima was first presented at the E-Poetry Festival 2009 in Barcelona and the voice we hear is reciting the poem *Schtzngrmm* by the Austrian poet Ernst Jandls (1925-2000).

The poem's title is a play with the German word "Schützengraben", which describes the trenches of the World War I. In the poem, Jandls describes the war by mimicking the sounds of gunfires and detonating missiles. Jandls was inspired by the Dada movement. In the book *Concrete*

Poetry: A World View, Mary Ellen Scott writes: "Jandl's traditional background enabled him to try 'to combine old and new elements' in his experimental poems". [2] In Tardón's video, we can also find this combination: the new virtual warfare from video games merges with Jandls "old" sound-poem from 1966 in a new exciting presentation.

Tardon's video reminds me the work of the American artist Joseph Delappe, who has performed poems reciting in different war games. In *War Poetry: Medal of Honor, Allied Assault Online*, Delappe reads anti-war poems by the WW1 poet Siegfried Sassoon. In Delappe's work, war video games become the ideal stage where to perform anti-war messages – in this case, a reaction against the war in Iraq that started in 2003. But already in 2001, Delappe started investigating on-line performances, reading Allen Ginsberg's famous poem *Howl* (1955) in the video game Elite Force Voyager Online. The reading took Delappe six hours to complete.

Artists and poets does not only use existing video games to bring poetry in them; some also create their own poetic video games. This is the case of the Canadian artist Jim Andrews, a pioneer in this area. In 2001, Andrews made a video game called *Arteroids* [3], a modification of Atari's classic Asteroids (1979). In the game, you steer a space ship through an asteroid belt, meanwhile you are shooting down asteroids and flying saucers. In Andrews' shoot-em-up poetry video game, you are steering a word and by shooting down other words you create a sound poetry. As a player, you interact and create the poem by the simple instructions: aim, fire, poetry!

Myfawny Ashmore, another Canadian artist, has made a series called *Gameboy Poetry* (2011). Ashmore describes her work as "game like poetry that exploit the relationship between the user, the hardware, the physicality of the user and the interface". In *TTC not a Haiku*, she combines scrollable TTC map with a poem, and in her work *Dear Sirs* she includes references to John Cage's famous poem *What you say*. [4]

The Australian digital artist and poet Jason Nelson (www.secret-technology.com) also creates his own poetry video games, like *Game, Game, Game And Again Game*, *I made this. You play this. We are Enemies* and *Evidence of everything exploding*. These video game poems are based on traditional platforms games in which Nelson combines texts, pictures and sounds from the different sources from the internet.

In the following interview, I asked Jason Nelson about the inspirations and the ideas behind his breathtaking game poetry.

Mathias Jansson: What kind of video games and poetry do you like, and what inspires you as an artist?

Jason Nelson: Lately I've been fascinated by the strange stories built into cut scenes and introductory movies of 1980s Atari or Nintendo games. The contrast between the relatively simple game play/graphics and the complex animated or image based storylines presented as rewards for defeating tentacled bosses. And while I doubt they were educated in the literary tradition, those who created early game narratives were pioneers. Their attempts to create small worlds and back-stories continue to be the inspiration for movies, games and novels thirty years later.

Additionally, those early games were often messy and dysfunctional with chaotic clashes of sounds and images. Without high powered graphics engines or developed AIs, the creators had to be creative within a limited framework. And so, I often scour the web for emulators and ROMS of any and all games systems. A project over the next year is to crack open ROMS for Space Adventure or Cute Animal platform games. Once inside I want to rewrite the rules or alter/disrupt the graphics. I imagine inserting acerbic poetic texts into Atari tennis games, or adding my own poorly filmed cut scenes into Sega Pirate Quests.

In a more modern vein, I'm always fascinated by how somewhat easy to use software, like Flash or GameMaker, is used to create an intimidating wide range of Indie games. Much of these would be considered outsider art.

As for poetry, I continually find myself pulling/creating poems from found texts. 19th century engineering journals, old medical documents, strange maps, diagrams of computer systems, which are filled with contemporary poetry. The language of science is often riddled with poetic descriptions or curious stories. Additionally, I create poetry through generative means.

Sometimes I filter movies, radio talk shows, political speeches through speech-to-text software. And because most code that translates sound into words is buggy and inconsistent, or filled with bias and predefined notions of language, the outcome of the filtered are pages of nearly incoherently grammars and word couplings. Often though, the textual relationships generated are beautiful and can be used to spark poetry within nearly all my creations. And of course, I am a voracious reader and explorer, so any poetry, fiction, creative non-fiction I can find ends up inspiring me in some way.

Creating digital poetry is so multi-linear and dimensional, and contains such a variety of media and poetic intersections that inspiration must come from all directions. As soon as I begin to create a new work, five new works seem to spring from the original idea. Critics often suggest some of my works seem incomplete either in their construction or in meaning. And I would say incompletion and messiness are part of the fabric of digital poetry.

How do you think the internet and video games have changed and will change how we read and experience poetry in the future?

Jason Nelson: Video Games are a language, an architecture for relaying ideas, for exploring some artistic / theoretical / poetic / educational / economic (and on and on) notions. The rise of relatively easy to code / create games unattached to profit / corporate directions, has meant game creators could use these architectures to communicate / build pretty and disturbing creatures. While I am overjoyed by the viral spreading my games have encountered, all my odd creations have accomplished is to slightly stretch how these frameworks could be used. Indeed, I am continually surprised by the creativity displayed in the independent gaming community.

And yet, I am equally shocked by how most big budget, platform specific works are, for the most part, un-creative and boring and over rely on fancy graphics. And even how we define "games" are constantly in revision. Maybe the term "game" no longer encapsulates what we create. If you can play / interact / solve / engage / rethink with an artwork, does that make it a game?

As for the future, interactive interfaces might not replace paper / static screen poetry. But, I am confident, interactive works will soon be a critical component of the literary landscape. The internet, portable devices, game consoles, are the language of Digital Natives. Anyone born after 1990 envisions content as interactive and multimedia, and each year after only increases their tendency to visual, spatial and responsive thinking.

Indeed, I've already seen signs of a backlash towards interactive poetry, and important signs of its impending dominance. Exactly how the poetry manifests itself will depend on the gadgets and codes developed. But in ten years, poetry will be written with interfaces, images, sounds, movements, databases, interactivity, game components all as vital as poetic texts.

Can you tell me something about your trilogy of poetic art games: *Game, Game and Again Game, I made this. You play this. We are enemies* and *Evidence of everything exploding*?

Jason Nelson: Most seem them as a trilogy. But I actually view most of my digital poetry creatures as game-like creations. Aside from the platform or top-down game engines, there is a slot-machine that predicts your death, generating a death scenario with each spin. I created a Zombie game, that while a failure in many ways does have the best title ever written (*Alarmingly these are not Lovesick Zombies*). Other works such as the within-within space of *Between Treacherous Objects,* the various cube creations, or the more fictional creations of *The Bomar Gene* or *Dreamaphage* or *Wittenoom,* all incorporate some game aspects. And one of my latest works, *Sydney's Siberia,* allows the user to infinitely explore a recombinatory mosaic of poetic tiles. It's a game of hide and seek with poetry that you can play forever. In addition, I've tried and failed with other game artworks, including a space shooter that takes 2 million minutes to play, or a soon to be released game that fills the screen with tombstones and short character bios of those killed during the game. So, while I understand why you might see a trilogy, I'm hoping it's more of a continually expanding experiment with interactive game-like poetic machines. And what is the difference between a machine and a creature?

What about *I made this, you play this, we are enemies*?

Jason Nelson: The title was a direct response to the thousands of emails / forum posts / blog entries about *Game, Game, Game And Again Game* that either loved it, or venomously hated it. That kind of polarized response, that strong visceral reaction is a great compliment to a creator, but at first the anger and aggression some expressed made me realize that combining two disparate art forms (poetry and games) meant I would ultimately make enemies in both camps. Some poets exclaimed my work wasn't truly literary and some game makers deemed by creations as easy-to-play artsy wankerism.

So, I created *I made this you play this we are enemies* using screenshots from many of the sites that promoted / lauded / lambasted my work. My idea was to mark-up or annotate the sites, to place a poetry game within net-based spaces, to combine sketchbook with commentary with absurd exploration. Although I am sure those addicted to the new-new of new media will cry out "same-same is lame-lame", I am planning to revisit the marked up screenshot poetry game platform. And instead of choosing popular sites, I'll be targeting relatively unknown portals, like the homepage for an Arboretum in Kansas or a small town museum in Vancouver, Canada or Toy Train collector's society, to bring digital poetry to local fanaticism.

Which role has the player / reader in your games?

Jason Nelson: Even the simple left / right / up arrow movement of my poetry games allow the reader to take the role of hero. To mentally live, however briefly, within the screen. And to varying degrees, within all my creations the reader / player truly does become the writer. No, I am not giving them complete control, nor am I generating texts from their movements and / or responses / reactions. The creator's ideas / aesthetic is still a strange attractor to all my digital creatures. It's almost as if I am offering them access to the back of my brain, letting them drive a lumbering hard to steer go-cart through poetic multimedia musings.

Evidence of everything exploding has a SF-story background about 10 important sheets of paper. Why these 10 papers and what are these levels represented in the game?

Jason Nelson: History, at least that history we study in school or experience through the media, is defined by seminal moments, is built from the evidence of seemingly important events. For *Evidence of everything exploding* I determined my own historical moments, signifiers of our contemporary condition. Perhaps it's best if I take you through all the levels, explaining, for the first time, how I chose the document for each.

One: the title page for an early etymological dictionary. Understanding the origin of language, the inspirations for terminologies is critical for poetic exploration. And the level story is centered on how language is used for dominating culture.

Two: an early Dadaism poster. As you've noticed, my work is usually heavily tinged with the surreal. The Dadaist movement, I feel, is the most influential thought movement of the 20th century. We force logic on what are inherently Alien systems.

Three: the trajectory diagram for NASA's first Moon landing. An obvious choice, at least on a personal level. As I am enamored with space travel and amazed at both the skill needed to travel to our nearest satellite, and saddened that for over thirty years we have yet to return.

Four: The Bill Gates Letter to Hobbyists from the Computer Brew Club newsletter. There was a moment when software turned bad, when code became commodity, when a language became copyright. This letter represents that sad change, the beginning of charging for hello.

Five: A 1918 US Gov't Warning Letter concerning the Spanish Flu pandemic. After the virus seemed unstoppable, there were plans drafted to isolate a small healthy population for the survival of humanity. The result of a multi-million killing virus was for communities to avoid large congregations for the next forty years.

Six: Copyright infringement notice to writer Neil Gaiman from the producers of *Attack of the Killer Tomatoes*. Pure absurdity and a narrow victory for public commentary. What if linking to a website you criticize was illegal.

Seven: a page from James Joyce. His odd confluence of words and ideas and strange inspired me to write, and began to rip fiction from its rusting cage.

Eight: NYC Museum of Modern Art rejection letter to pre-famous Andy Warhol. It's funny how success and fame alter a critic / curator's judgement. Personality / perception as conceptual underpinning to marginally interesting art.

Nine: Letter from a very young Fidel Castro praising America and seeking money. Rarely are megalomaniacs driven by anything other than ego. Politics are a malleable investment portfolio and one of oddest long-standing conflicts could have been avoided by a ten dollar investment.

Ten (the last level): the patent for the Pizza Box. Simple, ubiquitous and genius. A cultural symbol that just might outlast all the Face / My / Twit / Googs of the world. We are packaging for the easiest of foods.

First published on *Digimag*, Issue 63, April 2011, with the title "Aim, Fire, Poetry! Jason Nelson and the New Literatur".

[1] Cf. www.vimeo.com/4835713.
[2] Mary Ellen Scott, *Concrete Poetry: A World View*, Indiana University Press 1968.
[3] Cf. http://www.vispo.com/arteroids/.
[4] Cf. vimeo.com/16771373.

Martin Pichlmair

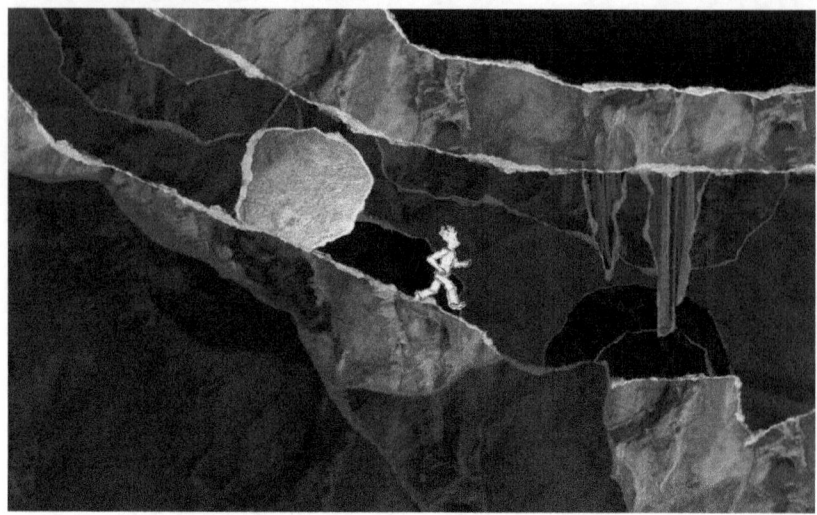

Broken Rules, *And Yet It Moves*, 2007. Screenshot

Martin Pichlmair has a doctoral degree in informatics, and has worked as assistant professor at the Institute of Design and Assessment of Technology at the Vienna University of Technology. Active for several years as a media artist, he has shown his work at various media art festivals and exhibitions, including the Ars Electronica Festival, ISEA, Transmediale and the Microwave Festival. In 2010 he joined Broken Rules (www.brokenrul.es), an independent game studio based in Vienna, Austria.

Mathias Jansson: You started as a new media artist but you then shifted focus from art to video games. Why?

Martin Pichlmair: One of the reasons why I wanted to shift to games is that I realized that those media art pieces I had created, that I was most happy with, were games in the first place. So there's not that much change in terms of content. What I lost is the critical attitude. The biggest difference is the audience. In media art you get 10 to maybe 300 specialists to see your piece. In games you have hundreds of thousands of "normal people".

In your artist's days, together with Fares Kayali, you created the *Bagatelle Concrete* (2006-2007), a pinball machine turned into a musical instrument. What was the concept behind this piece?

Martin Pichlmair: *Bagatelle Concrete* was a childhood dream come true. I wanted to create a pinball machine since I was maybe 5 or 6 years old. Instead of creating a new machine I bastardized an existing one in the best tradition of appropriation art. The idea was to deconstruct pinball until only the basic interactivity of play remains. That's why we removed the scoreboard. Adding music was an attempt at intensifying this kernel of play. It worked very well.

In the end, I don't mind in which medium I work. But while we've shown *Bagatelle Concrete* at a number of exhibitions, each of my released games has had more players than this art piece. It feels more relevant to bring some fresh air to the huge space of games than to cater to the delicate taste of art connoisseurs.

So, what's your opinion about games as art today?

Martin Pichlmair: Games are notoriously bad as "high art", just like comics, rap, photography, video art and street art. All these had to fight very hard to establish themselves as forms of art. The same is true for games. I'm not sure if becoming pieces of art is a worthy goal for games in the first place. Most people don't care about art.

You are working for Broken Rules, an independent game studio based in Vienna. What does Broken Rules focus on?

Martin Pichlmair: Our main strengths as a studio are attention to detail, a very democratic process and a certain disregard for conventions (hence the name). Most art pieces do not break many rules. Most games don't do so either. Personally I do not think that art is more than a label. It's an agreement and nothing else. The only thing that matters is if you touch your audience. So our main mission is to make games that offer meaningful interaction.

One of Broken Rules' recent games is *And Yet It Moves*. Can you tell me what is it that makes it stand out from other games in this genre?

Martin Pichlmair: When *And Yet It Moves* was first shown in public, in 2007, the genre of the puzzle platformer did not exist yet. Today, the game does not stand out as much as it did back then. The main feature of *And Yet It Moves* is that it breaks – or subverts – one rule of a very classic genre. It's a platformer where you have control over the direction of gravity. This tiny gameplay change resulted in a new experience of an old genre.

Finally, can you tell me something about *Chasing Aurora*, the game you are working on? What should the player expect this time from Broken Rules?

Martin Pichlmair: Our idea for *Chasing Aurora* is that we want to allow the player to experience the dream of flight. We're working hard to structure a game around this core experience. There will be multiplayer and singleplayer game modes and each will offer playful flight in a never experienced scenario. The game plays in the Alps at an unspecified time. We're aiming at something very magical – in an atavistic sense, not in the sense of colourful particle systems. You can expect a very unique game.

First published in *Next-Level* in April 2011 with the title "Martin Pichlmair from Broken Rules".

Rafäel Rozendaal

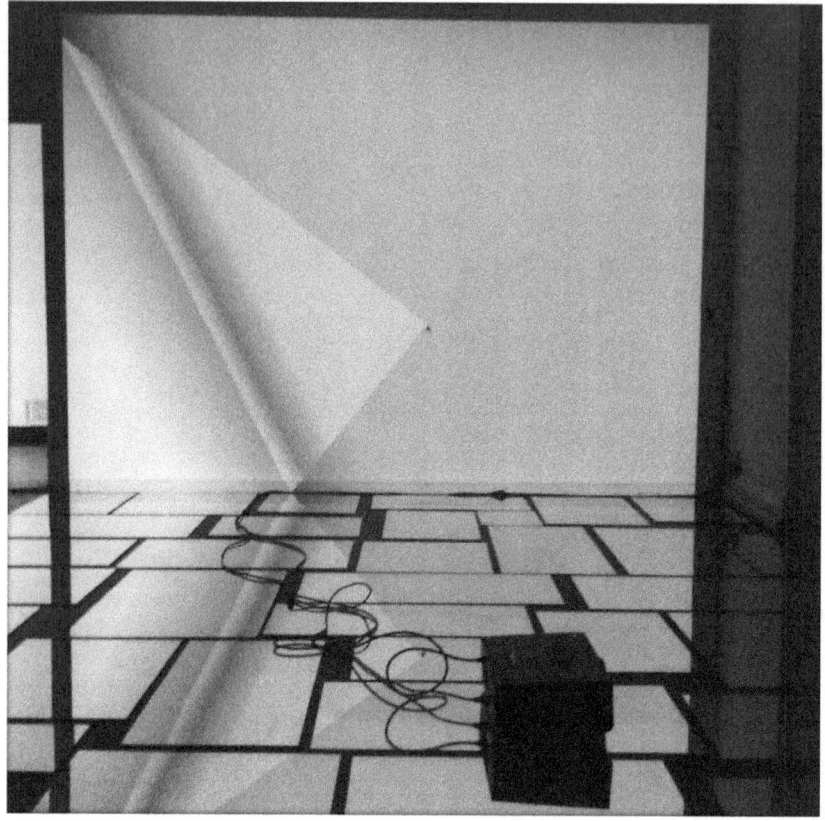

Rafael Rozendaal, *Color Flip*, 2008. Installation view at NIMk, Amsterdam. Photo Olof Werngren

In 2000, Miltos Manetas published the famous Neen Manifesto, in which he describes a new unidentified generation of artists that glorifies computers and artificial simulation, and that use the web as their gallery.

Two years later, Manetas and Peter Lunenfeld manifested the Neen concept in a spectacular "hijacking" of the Whitney Biennal domain name. A month before the opening of the biennal, the two friends discovered that the domain name Whitneybiennial.com was open for registration and they decided to challenge the museum show. After a well prepared media coup, they launched the new homepage with their own exhibition.

Around 20 artists were represented in the online biennial, including Miltos Manetas, Rafaël Rozendaal and Han Hooeerbrugge, and other "Neenstars" who presented artworks made in Macromedia Flash, the Neenstars' favourite palette.

On Whitneybiennial.com you could also find some theoretical texts [1]. Below you can find some important quotes that show what Neen was about:

"This generation does not care if their work is called art or design. This generation is no longer interested in the 'media critique' which preoccupied media artists of the last two decades; instead it is engaged in software critique." From "Generation Flash" by Lev Manovich

"Websites are today's most radical and important art objects." From "Websites, the art of our times" by Miltos Manetas

"Flash is PopTech, the OpArt of the new millennium. Flash is PoliTech, the irrepressible joy and lightness of being digital after the boom economy has gone bust." From "Flash is Poptech" by Peter Lunenfeld.

With Neen and Whitneybiennal.com, Flash was established as an artistic tool for a new generation of artists. Rafaël Rozendaal (www.newrafael.com) participated with *Why Was He Sad* (2002), a Flash work with a blue background, where big white clouds scrolled across the screen from left to right, and when you put you mouse over the clouds would burst with a "poff".

Today Rozendaal is a well established artist in the net art scene. Recently he participated in a commercial for the the new Nokia N9. When I saw it, Andy Warhol's Amiga commercial immediately came to my mind. When the home computer Amiga 500 was launched at a press conference in 1985, the Amiga market team invited Andy Warhol to paint Debbie Harry live on their computer. Maybe it's bold to compare Rozendaal with Warhol, but as you will see there are some interesting connections between Neen and Pop art.

Rozendaal fits well into the Neen concept. He mainly uses Flash in his work, he publishes all his work on the net and his art consists of web pages with unique domain names. But when I ask him if he calls himself a "Neenstar" and if he belongs to the "Flash generation", he replies that he rather wants to be connected with the Internet generation than to a particular manifesto or movement:

> Flash is a tool, but I care mostly about the internet. I belong to generation internet and Do It Yourself publishing. I am not waiting to be asked to take the initiative to explore the new landscape we all love, that is the internet.

Flash has always been an important tool for Rozendaal, as he confirms:

> I used Flash because it always works. In my experience all the other options (Javascript, frames, processing, CSS animation, DHTML, Shockwave, Silverlight, Canvas tag, WebGL, Unity) are either very different per browser or crash often. I always liked Flash because it is very reliable, and the files are tiny.

What will happen in the future with Flash? The last years developers have abandoned Flash in favour of the new HTML 5 standard, which has good support for video. Companies such as Apple don't support Flash in products like the iPad. Rozendaal's opinion is quite clear:

> We will see what happens. All the HTML5 demos I've checked behaved quite differently in different browsers and now Chrome is more optimized for SVG and Firefox for Canvas tag and lots of people don't update their browsers. I've made some iPhone apps and they have sold really well so that's great. It's nice to think about these mobile touch devices, and how people have them in their hands at all times. Whatever happens I'll go with the flow of technology, but I'm not a super early adapter. I wait till the mainstream is ready, because I like to speak to a large audience...

Since Whitneybiennal.com, Rozendaal has continued to develop his own artistic style. His works consist of large colorful fields and objects, sometimes with psychedelic effects. I think of Pop-art and Andy Warhol's famous screen prints of Marilyn Monroe when I see some of his works.

When I ask Raphael about his artistic inspiration, he answers that there are many different sources. The net is a big cut and paste inspiration area where you can mix everything with anything:

I love paintings, old cartoons, new cartoons, anything I love goes into my brain and becomes part of me. I like looking at things for a long time, staring, being bored, it's important.

Rafaël Rozendaal is a pure net artist, nearly every work of him is digital and available on the net. So it was a big surprise to find out that almost every work by Rozendaal begins with a handmade sketch before it goes digital.

I do the first drawings by hand because it's faster. I can make many and not worry and later I select which things to continue.

After the first drawing, the creative process continues through a number of steps:

Getting the idea, thinking, thinking, thinking some more, making a drawing, letting it rest, think more, take some photos, draw some more, google image, drawing, searching sounds online, looking for available domain names, letting it rest, meeting my programmer, see what's possible, drawing on computer, send to programmer, skype, skype, check first version, buy domain name, change settings in programming, skype more with programmer, finish it, publish with FTP, post on Facebook.

Many of Rozendaal's works are about repetition and motion. They can be walls that fall in a never ending loop, toilet paper that you can pull out for ever, doors that open new doors that open new doors and so on. In a way his works can be experienced as a metaphor of a never ending

Sisyphus work. A rather hopeless situation when you never get out of the loop, but on the other hand, you could also experience his works as a kind of meditative mantra that repeats itself and forces you to slow down and reflect. As he explains:

> I think it is a choice, I like making these moving images that do not have a beginning or end, but they still move, infinitely. Isn't it amazing that computers can create infinite generative images? I'm not sure why I do it or what it stands for, but it's something I have to do.

"Websites are today's most radical and important art objects", Miltos Manetas wrote. This is a statement that fits well with Rozendaal's work. When you buy one of his works, you not only buy a digital copy but also a unique art object, since every art work has a unique and exclusive domain name which the buyer purchases. To make it easier to sell his artworks, Rozendaal wrote a legal "Art Website Sales Contract":

> I made the contract because I needed it, because selling websites is a new thing so there were no examples yet. And since I made it I thought why not share it, so it can stimulate other artists to sell websites. I like the idea of art being open to the public yet exclusively owned. A piece of art that is everywhere in the world at the same time, isn't that amazing?

The digital also opens up new ways to exhibit art. Curator's Domenico Quaranta *MINI Museum of XXI Century Arts* (2010 – ongoing) is a 7" digital photo frame bought on eBay equipped with a 4GB pen drive. The MINI Museum then travels from node to node around a network of artists. [2] Artist's Aram Bartholl *Speed Show* [3] exhibition format consists of some simple instructions: "Hit an Internet-cafe, rent all computers they have and run a show on them for one night. All art works of the participating artists need to be on-line (not necessarily public) and are shown in a typical browser with standard plug-ins." Rozendaal has also explored exhibition formats inventing BYOB (Bring Your Own Beamer) [4]. BYOB is described as a series of one-night-exhibitions hosting artists and their projectors. This year, BYOB was selected by the Internet Pavillion at the Venice Biennal 2011. Rozendaal concludes explaining why BYOB is such a nice concept:

I am so happy with BYOB! BYOB is simple: find a place, invite many artists, ask them to bring their projector. It's open source, anyone can make a BYOB, and so it spreads fast. Within a year there were 48 editions all around the world. I think people make a lot of things online and this is an effective way of coming together and sharing that in a physical social environment, it makes people very happy.

First published on *Digimag*, issue 69, December 2011, with the title "Anything I Love Goes Into My Brain. An Interview With Rafael Rozendaal".

[1] Cf. www.manetas.com/eo/wb/files/theories.htm.
[2] Cf. http://minimuseum.linkartcenter.eu/.
[3] Cf. http://speedshow.net/.
[4] Cf. www.byobworldwide.com.

Jonatan Söderström

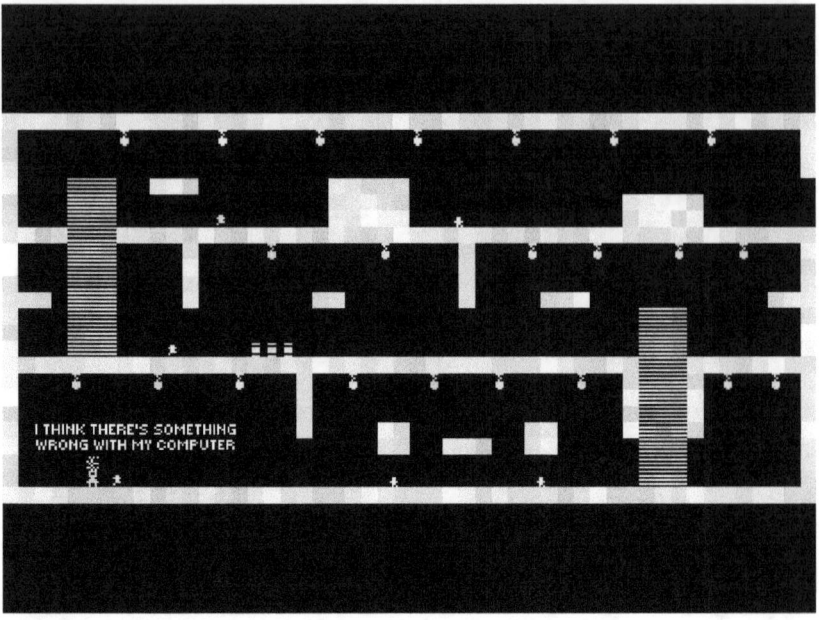

Cactus, *Evac*, 2012. Computer game, screenshot

Jonatan Söderström, also known as Cactus, is a Swedish independent game developer whose games could be described as experimental and artistic. His small characteristic games are often created in a short period of time. *Life is a Race* (2008) took only 2 hours to complete, *Stench Mechanics* and *Lovecraft Game* (2008) took a day to finish. On his blog, you can find this statement: "I've been making small freeware games since 2004. My aim is to create interesting things, whether it be through visuals or gameplay mechanics. A lot of the games on my site are just small experiments dressed up as games."

Mathias Jansson: When did you start making your own games? Where do you find inspiration?

Jonatan Söderström: I started making games when I was eighteen, I think. I just wanted to do something creative and didn't really feel like I got the response I wanted when I attempted to make music or draw comics. I didn't think that you could make games on your own if you didn't have some form of education in programming, so I was happy to find tools that let me do games without any real programming. It really felt nice being able to design your own little worlds, so I kept doing it for a while without really showing anyone what I was making. Then I found communities on the web where people were really supportive and appreciative of what I was doing.

I found out that the games that people were making felt differently from what you normally see in mainstream games. They were the ones that appealed the most to me and they also felt fairly simple to create, so I kept doing odd small sized projects for a while, without really thinking about the purpose and meaning they had. Then I started getting into weird movies and was overwhelmed by how interesting it was to experience things that generally felt alien and strange; that people can make things that I don't understand at all but somehow make sense in their own weird way. David Lynch and Jodorowsky were big influences, and I also really enjoyed reading manga by authors like Junji Ito, Shintaro Kago and a bunch of others that targeted a more mature audience. So I figured out that it was something I wanted to do as well.

Game developers can spend months and years to make a game, but your games are often made in a very short time. Why?

Jonatan Söderström: There are many reasons to work as fast as I do. I have a short attention span and easily get bored of the projects I'm working on. All the ideas I have aren't suitable for longer projects either, and if you release more games you get more attention. If you only make big games you have to sacrifice a lot of cool ideas that you simply don't have the time to explore.

What's your take on the distrubution possibilities of indie games?

Jonatan Söderström: There's basically only downloadable content from Steam, XBLA or PSN that seems viable right now. If you have a fanbase big enough you can try to sell games on your own site, but it's a lot harder. You can also sell your soul and use ads, or do online games with subscriptions I guess, but I doubt I'll ever do that.

Can you tell me about the game Norrland that you made for an exhibition in Sweden 2010?

Jonatan Söderström: It's based on the prejudice that exists around the people who live up north. Basically I just wanted to piss people off, but at the same time make a game that had a dark and serious subtone. I've also been saying that games don't have to be fun to be good, and I think *Norrland* is a good example of that.

Would you describe your games as art?

Jonatan Söderström: Well, yes. I'm not a pretentious person but I don't think that what I'm doing is nothing more than entertainment. I want to do interesting things for interesting people, but I rarely try to emphasize on the "art" aspect in my games, it's just a part of some projects that I want to use to create a feeling of depth that may or may not be there.

First published in *Next-Level* in December 2011 with the title "Cactus alias Jonatan Söderström".

Jeroen D. Stout

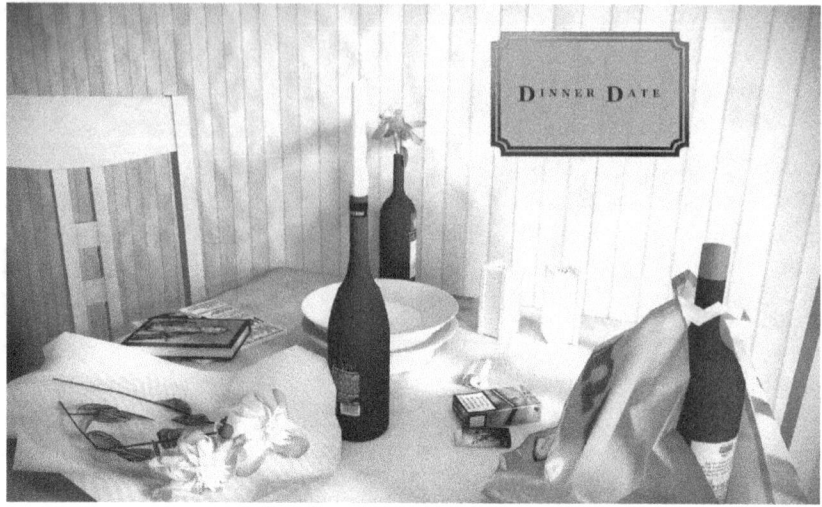

Jeroen D. Stout, *Dinner Date*, 2010. Promotional image

"You play as the subconsciousness of Julian Luxemburg, waiting for his date to arrive. You listen in on his thoughts while tapping the table, looking at the clock and eventually reluctantly starting to eat…" Well, it doesnt't seems much of a story for a video game, but Jeroen D. Stout's indie game *Dinner Date* let's you play a psychological experience of the main character in an interesting way The game could be described as a combination of video game narrative and theatre performance, in which you play the main character Julian Luxemburg from a First Person Shooter view.

Mathias Jansson: What inspires you as an artist and game designer?

Jeroen D. Stout: I mostly draw inspiration from people I meet and the arts I truly enjoy - 19th century painting, music and literature. It's easy with games to get sucked into the bubble of 'games as way of life', but I think day-to-day life and the arts are unmissable. I believe that all good ideas are composed of 'borrowed' smaller ideas and that an artist can do nothing worse than limit himself to one closed 'scene'. When watching films or reading novels I do find that I stockpile small ideas that I hope will come out when I am making work myself.

There is a certain 'sense of life' you can get from art which is not directly a set of facts, but rather an experience that gives you an 'understanding' of a scene, situation or even country. Reading literature from different nations I find that the very way people think wildly differs in very beautiful ways – something I personally tremendously enjoy. These are all feelings and sensations which you could rarely stumble upon in daily life, and art can teach you how to find them.

I find I compose my artistic work with a form of empathy; a little pocket universe which I can believe in, that showcases some intriguing combination of ideas.

Your biggest success is the game *Dinner Date*, which has been recognised and nominated for the IGF award. What is it that makes it so special?

Jeroen D. Stout: *Dinner Date* does not adhere to the common idea that in a game you drive the action, or that the game is battling against you. Rather, you sit at a kitchen table listening to a man's thoughts as he waits for a date, while doing his subconscious actions; tapping the table, looking at the clock, eating bread. This comes from a more theatrical angle: the idea for an actor is to be the embodiment of a character, and in that way take a script and make it emotive.

Dinner Date was a first step to get players to pretend they are the main character on a more theatrical level. Because I do this, I can write the story more like a play, so I can construct a character arc and expect it to be played out in a certain way. It is very liberating in terms of narrative, but still inviting to a player who wants to be part of it.

What about the leading character, Julian Luxemburg?

Jeroen D. Stout: Julian Luxemburg is a man whose perception of himself seems to hinge on a date. He ultimately has several questions and problems with the way he sees life, and the game is ultimately about unravelling this; trying to figure out why Julian is who he is, and why he is so hell-bent on getting a date.

I always considered the end of *Dinner Date* the end of the character as far as my writing goes; I wrote him enough to sustain the arc of *Dinner Date* but I think he is in that sense a puzzle that makes sense when you solve him; and after that you no longer need any further puzzle pieces.

I am working on a new game with two new characters, which is very exciting, as I can do the same trickery and slowly reveal who they really are throughout the game – show not what they do but who they are.

What about the Dutch indie game scene? Last year, the Stedelijk Museum in Amsterdam has worked with artists and game designers. Do you feel that art games are recognised as an art form in the Netherlands?

Jeroen D. Stout: I know the Netherlands are quite fond of its indie scene – there is a tremendous amount of schools and a lively group of people. But I must admit I am no longer sure what it means to be 'recognised as an art form'. Sometimes people on game forums are very open to 'art games' and sometimes the contemporary art scene is open to games, but in a way which to me makes it questionable whether they even understand games. I spend most of my time away from contemporary art scenes because, frankly, I find it mostly incoherent and meaningless. The 'badge of honour' that the word art implies is not something I even care to receive from the current art scene.

My own frame of reference is the likes of Bouguereau, Hugo or Tchaikovsky; and what I'm working towards is to make work that may be judged on that level. As to who will do this judging I am not sure – but I speak with many people who wouldn't mind an 'academic' revival, and perhaps games will ultimately be an essential part of this.

And what do you think about the future of indie games?

Jeroen D. Stout: Ultimately, I think it will simply take 'time' to build the infrastructure. At the moment everybody I meet knows about computer games at least second hand. In a few decades there will be a tremendous group of people who play games and who know how to find them; and the whole way in which we finance things may have changed away from requiring the big publishers. Digital distribution and crowd-financing along with a public that is aware in how they may find things will ultimately make it possible, I think, for small teams to make small things for a selected group, and finance their lives with it.

First published in *Next-Level* in February 2012 with the title "Jeroen D. Stout from Stout Games".

Erik Svedäng

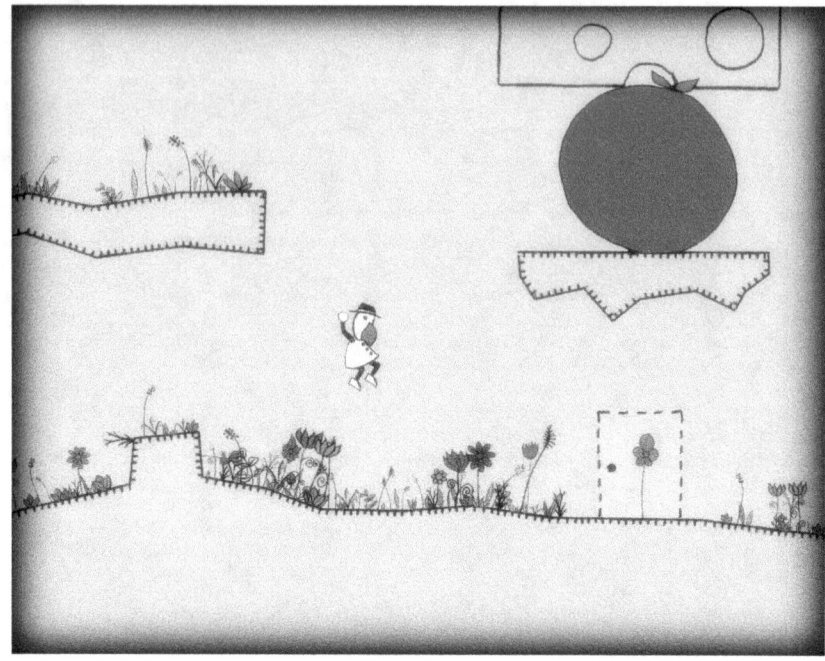

Erik Svedäng, *Blueberry Garden*, 2008. Computer game, screenshot

Born in Uppsala, Sweden, in 1986, Erik Svedäng (http://erik-svedang.com) is an indie game developer currently based in Gothenburg, Sweden. In 2009, his game *Blueberry Garden* won the IGF Seamus McNally Grand Prize.

Mathias Jansson: When did you start making your own games?

Erik Svedäng: I started making board games when I was 4 or 5, after my cousins showed me that it was a possible thing to do. When I got older I learned how to program and made simple games for me and my friends.

Where do you find inspiration for your games?

Erik Svedäng: I am usually very much inspired by music, but also from what I read or experience. I like to go for walks and think, so I think the nature around me influences me a lot. For *Blueberry Garden* it was the archipelago; for my new big project it is the city of Gothenburg where I currently live.

In the game Kometen you collaborated with Swedish artist Niklas Åkerblad. How important is for you the artistic quality of the graphics in your games?

Erik Svedäng: It's very important! I like to collaborate with different people to bring different things into my work. And also because it's fun to work together of course.

Your game *Shot Shot Shoot* was developed for iPad. How did the advent of smartphones and handheld devices affect you as a game developer?

Erik Svedäng: I really like the idea of electronic board games; things that bring people together by using these new interfaces. Classic console and PC gaming is great too but it is so focused on watching the monitor. I like the tension that comes from facing your opponent in real life.

Your latest project is called *Clairvoyance*. Can you tell me something about it?

Erik Svedäng: It started off as a normal board game with wooden cubes. I wanted to make height be of great importance, so I let the players stack these cubes on top of each other. To make the game go faster and be more intense I let both players plan their moves simultaneously and then reveal them, which made the rules end up very much like a 3D version of Robo Rally + Chess. When I showed the game to my team mates (who I am working with on another, bigger game) they liked it a lot so we tried to make a quick little computer version of it. Of course it took much longer than planned but hopefully we can release it to the public soon (it's in closed beta at the time).

What do you think about the future of indie games?

Erik Svedäng: I am hopeful for the future. I'm very frugal at the moment so it works out somehow. Hopefully the games I'm working on now will find an audience and let me continue. It seems like most people who make great things in the indie game world actually manage to get by, so that's promising!

First published in *Next-Level* in March 2012 with the title "Shot Shot Shoot: Interview with Erik Svedäng".

Anders Weberg

YOU ARE WATCHING A COPY OF 101010 IT WAS UPLOADED ON THE P2P NETWORKS 2010/10/10 THE ORGINAL FILM AND ALL THE MATERIAL USED TO CREATE IT IS DELETED IT WILL ONLY EXIST AS LONG AS IT'S SHARED.	SHARE THIS FILM FOR AS LONG AS YOU LIKE OR DELETE IT IMMEDIATELY THE AESTHETICS OF EPHEMERALITY WWW.P2P-ART.COM SINCE 2006 BY ANDERS WEBERG WWW.WEBERG.SE

Anders Weberg, Two screenshots from *101010*, 2010.

These six following URLs are art. No, I don't mean that the URLs lead to an homepage with a net art project. I mean that the URL itself is the artwork.

http://www.theurlistheartwork.com/
http://you-talking-to-me.com/
http://lrntrlln.org/p/thisisart/
http://canyoubelievethisdomainwasavailable.com/
http://asdflkjhasdflkjhasdflkjhasdflkjhasdflkjhasdflkjhasdflkj.com/
http://www.thissiteisnotavailableinyourcountry.com/

Web based art must have an address, an URL, which tells the user where the artwork is stored on the web. Among others, Swedish artist Anders Weberg took this obvious, but inescapable fact as the starting point for a work of art.

So, If you digit www.theurlistheartwork.com in your browser you will be taken to a page with the text: "*The url is The artwork* by Anders Weberg, October 2009". Can a net based artwork be more minimalistic and sublime?

The artist duo Jodi have already used this technique to create net art. If you surf to the address http://you-talking-to-me.com/, you will find the following monologue, which constantly repeats itself in the browser address bar:

http://you-talking-to-me.com/
http://well-i-am-the-only-one-here.com/
http://who-the-fuck-do-you-think-you-are-talking-to.com/
http://you-talking-to-me-you-talking-to-me-you-talking-to-me.com/
http://then-who-the-hell-else-are-you-talking-to.com/

The monologue is taken from the movie *Taxi Driver* (1976) in which

Travis Bickle (played by Robert de Niro) stands before a mirror and talks to himself. Jodi lets the monologue repeat itself ad infinitum just by sending the visitors around a loop of different URLs.

Sumoto.iki, a French net artists, is the author of the page *This is art*. The URL leads you to a white page with a text saying: "This is a page. Just click everywhere". The text "This is a page" refers to a painting by he famous surrealist artist René Magritte (1898- 1967), who used to play with words in his titles. The painting *La trahison des images* (1929) is well known in art history because the painting shows a pipe, but the caption says it's not a pipe, because it's not a real pipe, but only the image of a pipe. When sumoto.iki says "This is a page", he is right, but the URL also says "This is art" and since sumoto.iki is an artist the statement seems legitimate. The URL, the title, makes an ordinary web page a piece of art.

The URL is the core of the Internet and it's vital to have an easy and catchy URL that the visitors can remember. Misspelled URLs of well-known domain names are often used by non serious people to earn money, but artists can also use URLs to make art. A unique and different URL can make the visitor start thinking about what an URL is and why we use them.

Artist David Kraftsows' work http://canyoubelievethisdomainwas-available.com leads the visitor to a white homepage with the text: "Can you believe this domain was available???" The answer is of course yes. Who would like to register a domain that people won't remember?

Evan Roth has taken this question to the ultimate limit. His online web based new work is a very hard URL to spell (http://asdflkjhasdflkjh-asdflkjhasdflkjhasdflkjhasdflkjhasdflkjhasdflkj.com), but when you finally succeed to reach the page you are warmly rewarded. You can always cheat and click on the link, but then you miss a vital part of the work, which is the manual typing of the URL. A process that is so important for the work that Roth has created an URL performance available on Vimeo (http://vimeo.com/1140419).

But let us return to Anders Weberg (born 1968), living in Malmö Sweden and working as an artist and experimental filmmaker. He has become known to a broader public by using P2P technique as his gallery and distribution channel for video art. Weberg is a frequent guest at different film festivals and New Media art events all around the world.

One of his latest films, *Sweden for beginners* (made in collaboration with Robert Willim), is an imaginative journey through the spaces, the life and everyday world of Sweden, investigating stereotypes of Sweden, like the Bergmanesque gloom, erotica and nature romanticism.

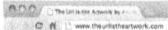

Anders Weberg, *The URL Is the Artwork*, 2009

Weberg's interest in places is also the subject for *Elsewhereness*, a series of videos made from audio and video material found on the web that emanates from a specific city like Utrecht, Cape Town, Manchester or Yokohama."The audiovisual pieces are manipulated and composed into a surreal journey through an estranged landscape, based entirely on the culturally bound and stereotypical preconceptions of the artists about the actual location", Weberg explains.

Along the last years Weberg also started making net art and URL-art as mentioned above. The following interview focuses on this recent body of work.

Mathias Jansson: When did your interest for net art and P2P start?

Anders Weberg: I started to conceive this project in the late-90s and when I had just started using the Internet for publishing videos. In the same time "Napster" happened. The P2P Art project was release in 2006 and could be described as: "Art made for – and only available on – the peer to peer networks. The original artwork is first shared by the artist until one other user has downloaded it. After that the artwork will be available for as long as other users share it. The original file and all the material used to create it are deleted by the artist. There's no original".

Basically I make films that are uploaded and shared on the P2P nets, while original files are deleted forever. The shared works start their new, autonomous life, surfing the Net without any control, in a compressed low-resolution version. When people stop sharing the films, they are gone forever. On one hand it's a way to acknowledge the beauty of work that is existing only briefly. This has been done many times before in the art world history using different media and methods. On the other hand it's a comment to the precious original.

Also, we currently exist in an era where almost everything is within keyboard reach, and, at the same time, we desire things that are not easily accessible. That is part of human nature.

So in a way the project is about creating scarcity with the same technology that is intended to make information readily accessible and reproducible.

Up until now five films have been released and deleted. The shortest was 45 minutes and the longest was the nine hour, nine minutes, nine seconds and nine frames long film that I released 2009/09/09, *090909*. The next release will be *101010* released on 2010/10/10.

In 2009 you made a net art work called *The URL is the Artwork*. How did you come up with the idea?

Anders Weberg: At that time I had done some net projects together with Artist and Cultural Analysist Robert Willim, where we included GPS devices, Google Earth and digital video, and I was looking for a more clean net art project. I was trying to be as minimalistic as I could think of at that time.

What does the URL mean for you as an artist?

Anders Weberg: It does mean a lot to me. Identity perhaps? Perhaps today an URL is more important than a gallery. Can a URL be a gallery? Is there a need for a gallery if you are making work that fits in a URL? These are interesting and challenging times to be an artist. Today the boundaries between online / offline are blurred and I'm always curious on how new technologies are used by the public and how that can be transformed into my own work.

As a sidenote, I lost the most valuable asset I have (or had) a month ago when my domain www.andersweberg.com was lost because I missed to re-register it and someone bought it. Since then, I've been taking screenshots of the new site every day, with its ads for small blue pills and machines that will make your manhood grow. Perhaps that will lead to another project.

Is there any similarity between your URL-art and your P2P-art? Which ideas or concept do you like to explore or discuss in your art?

Anders Weberg: I think the common denominator in my more concept based art is meant to comment upon and raise questions around issues of authorship, fair use, copyright, attribution, citation, accreditation, intellectual property, censorship and consumerism.

Anders Weberg, *This Site Is Not Available in Your Country*, 2010.

In your latest www.thissiteisnotavailableinyourcountry.com, the user finds a statement similar to the one that sites as YouTube present when there are copyright or censorship restrictions...

Anders Weberg: Yes. The project also comments on the so called "freedom" of the net, that we take for granted but that's not the case in all countries.

What do you think about copyright as an artist?

Anders Weberg: I do think the "precious" original always will have a place in a lot of people hearts, but today most of us treat all kinds of media very ephemeral without that much care about the precious original when everything is available and free online. Is there a real difference bewteen the original and its exact replica as a digital copy?

Many things have been written about these issues but for me the eye opener was back when I started working with computers and realized that if I pushed CTRL/CMD + c and CTRL/CMD + v I had a perfect copy of the original file. In the age of contents sharing through the Net, in fact, we always find ourselves in a new condition of resources ubiquity, always disposable in a million of versions indistinguishable one to another: an army of multiples without an original. As an artist and given the kind of work I do I think it's pretty clear how I feel about copyright on my own work. All rights reserved. All wrongs reversed.

First published in *Digimag,* issue 59, November 2010, with the title "Anders Weberg. Url And Networks As Artworks".

www.janssonswebb.se

www.ingramcontent.com/pod-product-compliance
Lightning Source LLC
Chambersburg PA
CBHW060850170526
45158CB00001B/300